— *Great Themes of the Bible* —

COMMUNITY:

You Will Be My Witnesses

Timothy Merrill

ABINGDON PRESS

NASHVILLE

GREAT THEMES OF THE BIBLE
Community: You Will Be My Witnesses
By Timothy Merrill

ISBN 0-687-34313-5

This book is printed on recycled, acid-free, and elemental-chlorine–free paper.

MANUFACTURED IN THE UNITED STATES OF AMERICA

05 06 07 08 09 10 11 12 13 14—10 9 8 7 6 5 4 3 2 1

Table of Contents

Welcome to
Great Themes of the Bible

We are pleased that you have chosen *Great Themes of the Bible* for your small-group study. This series of study books cultivates faith formation in contemporary life using reliable principles of Christian education to explore major themes of the Bible, the issues and questions generated by these themes, and how the Bible illuminates our response to them in daily life. The sessions provide many opportunities for spiritual growth through worship, study, reflection, and interaction with other participants.

Great Themes of the Bible Cultivates Faith Formation in Contemporary Life

Who is God? How is God at work in our world? How does God call us and relate to us? How do we relate to God and to one another? What does Jesus Christ reveal to us about God? What is the potential for life in which we choose to be committed to God through Jesus Christ? How do we find hope? Such questions are at the heart of faith formation in contemporary life.

The Bible presents great themes that are universally relevant for the faith formation of all human beings in all times and places. Great themes such as call, creation, covenant, Christ, commitment, and community provide points of encounter between contemporary life and the times, places, and people in the Bible. As we reflect upon faith issues in our daily lives, we can engage biblical themes in order to learn more about God and in order to interpret what it means to live with faith in God.

The great themes of the Bible are the great themes of life. They generate questions and issues today just as they did for those in the biblical world. As we identify and explore these themes, we also engage the related questions and issues as they emerge in our contemporary life and culture. Exploring the Bible helps us see how people in the biblical world dealt with the issues and questions generated by a particular theme. Sometimes they responded exactly the way we would respond. Other times, they responded quite differently. In every case, however, we can glimpse God at work as we compare and contrast their situations with our own.

In Christian faith formation, we delve again and again into the Bible as we reflect upon our daily lives in light of Christian teaching. One way to imagine this process is by envisioning a spiral. A theme in the Bible generates questions and issues. We reflect upon the theme and consider the questions and issues it raises in our contemporary lives. We read the Bible and ask ourselves how the stories and teachings inform the theme and its questions and issues. We reflect upon the insights we have gained and perhaps make adjustments in our lives. We spiral through a particular theme and its issues and questions more than once as we look to the Bible for help, guidance, and hope. As we participate in this ongoing process, we gain deeper awareness of who God is and what God wants us to do, to be, and to become. The books in the *Great Themes of the Bible* series are structured around this spiraling process of faith formation.

Theme

Bible

Issues and
Questions in
Contemporary Life

Great Themes of the Bible Is Built Upon Reliable Christian Education Principles

The sessions in each of the books in *Great Themes Of The Bible* are based on the Scriptures and lesson guides in the *Uniform Series of International Bible Lessons for Christian Teaching*. These guides provide reliable Christian education principles to those who write the books. Session development for a book in *Great Themes of the Bible* is guided by a unifying principle that illuminates the unity between life and the Bible by emphasizing a key theme. The principle contains three components: a life statement, a life question, and a biblical response.

The lesson guides in the Uniform Series also include statements for every Scripture that help the writer to think about and develop the sessions. These statements occur in five categories or matrices: Learner, Scripture, Faith Interaction, Teaching Strategies, and Special Interest.

Statements in the Learner matrix identify general characteristics describing life stages, developmental issues, and particular experiences (special needs, concerns, or celebrations) that characterize learners.

Statements in the Scripture matrix identify a variety of key issues, questions, practices, and affirmations raised from the biblical texts. These may include historical, cultural, ethical, and theological perspectives.

Statements in the Faith Interaction matrix identify ways in which learners and Scripture might interact in the context of the Bible study. The statements relate to personal, communal, and societal expressions of faith.

Statements in the Teaching Strategies matrix suggest ways for writers to create sessions that connect Scripture and learners through a variety of educational methods that take into account the different ways people learn.

Statements in the Special Interest matrix identify ways writers might address topics of special concern that are particularly appropriate to the Scripture text: handicapping conditions, racial and ethnic issues, drug and alcohol abuse, and ecology, for example.

While the Faith Interaction matrix provides the beginning point for each session in a book in the *Great Themes of the Bible,* learning goals employed by the writers arise from all these matrices.

Great Themes of the Bible Provides Opportunities for Spiritual Growth

The books in *Great Themes of The Bible* offer you an opportunity to see the vital connection between daily life and the Bible. Every session begins and ends with worship in order to help you experience God's presence as you participate in the sessions. The small group sessions also provide opportunities to develop friendships with others that are based upon respect, trust, and mutual encouragement in faith formation.

The following principles guide our approach to spiritual growth and faith formation:

- Faith and life belong together. We seek to discover connections or crossing points between what God reveals in the Bible and the needs, choices, and celebrations of our ordinary experience. Biblical themes provide this crossing point.
- Everyone is a theologian. *Theology* may be defined as "loving God with our minds" as well as with our hearts. All in your group, regardless of background, are fully qualified to do that.
- Adults learn best through reflection on experience. No longer are we blank tablets on which new knowledge must be imprinted. We can draw on a fund of experiences, and ask what it means for us in light of Scripture and Christian teaching about God and creation.
- Questions stimulate spiritual growth more than answers. An authoritative answer seems final and discourages further thinking, while a stimulating question invites further creative exploration and dialogue.
- Learning involves change, choice, and pain. If we are to take seriously what God is telling us in Scripture, we must be open to changing our opinions, making new lifestyle choices, and experiencing the pain of letting go of the old and moving into a new and unknown future, following the God of continuing creation.
- Community sharing fosters spiritual growth. When a group commits to struggling together with questions of faith and life, they share personal experiences, challenge assumptions, deepen relationships, and pray. God's Spirit is present. The God of continuing creation is at work.

We pray that you will experience the freedom to ask questions as you explore the great themes in your life and in the Bible. We pray that you will encounter and experience the life-transforming love of God as you become part of a *Great Themes of the Bible* group. And finally, we pray that you will see yourself as a beloved human being created in the image of God and that you will grow in your love of God, self, and neighbor.

Using the Books in
Great Themes of the Bible

Each book in the *Great Themes of the Bible* series has within its pages all you need to lead or to participate in a group.

At the beginning of each book you will find:

- suggestions for organizing a *Great Themes of the Bible* small group.
- suggestions for different ways to use the book.
- suggestions for leading a group.
- an introduction to the great theme of the Bible that is at the center of all the sessions.

In each of the seven sessions you will find:

- a focus statement that illuminates the particular issues and questions of the theme in contemporary life and in the Scriptures for the session.
- opening and closing worship experiences related to the focus of each session.
- concise, easy-to-use leader/learner helps placed in boxes near the main text to which they refer.
- main content rich with illustrations from contemporary life and reliable information about the Scriptures in each session.

In the Appendix you will find:

- a list of Scriptures that illuminate the biblical theme.
- information about The Committee on the Uniform Series.
- information about other Bible study resources that may interest your group.

Books in the *Great Themes of the Bible* series are designed for versatility of use in a variety of settings.

Small Groups on Sunday Morning. Sunday morning groups usually meet for 45 minutes to an hour. If your group would like to go into greater depth, you can divide the sessions and do the study for longer than seven weeks.

Weekday or Weeknight Groups. We recommend 60 to 90 minutes for weekday/weeknight groups. Participants should prepare ahead by reading the content of the session and choosing one activity for deeper reflection and study. A group leader may wish to assign these activities.

A Weekend Retreat. For a weekend retreat, distribute books at least two weeks in advance. Locate and provide additional media resources and reference materials, such as hymnals, Bibles, Bible dictionaries and commentaries, and other books. If possible, have a computer with Internet capabilities on site. Tell participants to read their study books before the retreat. Begin on Friday with an evening meal or refreshments followed by gathering time and worship. Review the introduction to the theme. Do the activities in Session 1. Cover Sessions 2, 3, 4, 5, and 6 on Saturday. Develop a schedule that includes time for breaks, meals, and personal reflection of various topics and Scriptures in the sessions. Cover Session 7 on Sunday. End the retreat with closing worship on Sunday afternoon.

Individual Devotion and Reflection. While the books are designed for small-group study, they can also be beneficial for individual devotion and reflection. Use the book as a personal Bible study resource. Read the Scriptures, then read the main content of the sessions. Adapt the questions in the leader/learner boxes to help you reflect upon the issues related to the biblical theme. Learning with a small group of persons offers certain advantages over studying alone. In a small group, you will encounter people whose life experiences, education, opinions and ideas, personalities, skills, talents, and interests may be different from yours. Such differences can make the experience of Bible study richer and more challenging.

Organizing a *Great Themes of the Bible* Small Group

Great Themes of the Bible is an excellent resource for all people who are looking for meaning in their daily lives, who want to grow in their faith, and who want to read and reflect upon major themes in the Bible. They may be persons who are not part of a faith community yet who are seekers on a profound spiritual journey. They may be new Christians or new members who want to know more about Christian faith. Or they may be people who have been in church a long time but who feel a need for spiritual renewal. All such persons desire to engage more deeply with issues of faith and with the Bible in order to find meaning and hope.

Great Themes of the Bible is an excellent small-group study for those who have completed *Beginnings,* a program that introduces the basics of Christian faith. It is ideal for those who are not yet involved in an ongoing Bible study, such as *Adult Bible Studies*, DISCIPLE, *Genesis to Revelation,* and *Journey Through the Bible,* or for those who prefer short-term rather than long-term studies. *Great Themes of the Bible* also provides a point of entry for those who have never been involved in any kind of Bible study.

Starting a *Great Themes of the Bible* study group is an effective way to involve newcomers in the life of your local church. If you want to start a *Great Themes of the Bible* small group as part of the evangelism program in your local church, follow the steps below:

- Read through the *Great Themes of the Bible* study book. Think about the theme, the issues generated by the theme, and the Scriptures. Prepare to respond to questions that someone may ask about the study.

- Develop a list of potential participants. An ideal size for a small group is 7 to 12 people. Your list should have about twice your target number (14 to 24 people). Have your local church purchase a copy of the study book for each of the persons on your list.

- Decide on a location and time for your *Great Themes of the Bible* group. Of course, the details can be negotiated with those persons who accept the invitation; but you need to sound definitive and clear to prospective group members. "We will initially set Wednesday night from 7 to 9 P.M. at my house for our meeting time" will sound more attractive than "Well, I don't know either when or where we would be meeting; but I hope you will consider joining us."

• Identify someone who is willing to go with you to visit the persons on your list. Make it your goal to become acquainted with each person you visit. Tell them about *Great Themes of the Bible*. Give them a copy of the study book for this group. Even if they choose not to attend the small group at this time, they will have an opportunity to read the book on their own. Tell each person the initial meeting time and location and how many weeks the group will meet. Invite them to become part of the group. Thank them for their time.

• Publicize the new *Great Themes of the Bible* study through as many channels as are available. Announce it during worship. Print notices in the church newsletter and bulletin and on the church Web site if you have one. Use free public event notices in community newspapers. Create flyers for mailing and posting in public places.

• A few days before the session begins, give a friendly phone call or send an e-mail to thank all persons you visited for their consideration and interest. Remind them of the time and location of the first meeting.

For more detailed instructions about starting and maintaining a small group, read *How to Start and Sustain a Faith-based Small Group*, by John D. Schroeder (Abingdon, 2003).

Leading a *Great Themes of the Bible* Small Group

A group may have one leader for all the sessions, or leadership may be rotated among the participants. Leaders do not need to be experts in Bible study because the role of the leader is to facilitate discussion rather than to impart information or teach a particular content. Leader and learner use the same book and share the same commitment to read and prepare for the *Great Themes of the Bible* session each week. So what does the leader actually do?

A Leader Prepares for the Session

Pray. Ask for God's guidance as you prepare to lead the session.

Read. Read the session and its Scriptures ahead of time. Jot down questions or insights that occur during the reading. Look at the leader/learner helps in the boxes.

Think about group participants. Who are they? What life issues or questions might they have about the theme? about the Scriptures?

Prepare the learning area. Gather any needed supplies, such as sheets of newsprint, markers, paper and pencils, Bibles, hymnals, audio-visual equipment, masking tape, a Bible dictionary, Bible commentaries, a Bible atlas. If you are meeting in a classroom setting, arrange the chairs in a circle or around a table. Make sure that everyone will have a place to sit.

Prepare a worship center. Find a small table. Cover it with an attractive cloth. Place a candle in a candleholder on the center. Place matches nearby to light the candle. Place on the worship center a Bible or other items that relate to or illuminate the session focus.

Pray. Before the participants arrive, pray for each one. Ask for God's blessing on your session. Offer thanks to God for the opportunity to lead the session.

A Leader Creates a Welcoming Atmosphere

Hospitality is a spiritual discipline. A leader helps create an environment that makes others feel welcome and that helps every participant experience the freedom to ask questions and to state opinions. Such an atmosphere is based upon mutual respect.

Greet participants as they arrive. Say their names. If the group is meeting for the first time, use nametags.

Listen. As group discussion unfolds, affirm the comments and ideas of participants. Avoid the temptation to dominate conversation or "correct" the ideas of other participants.

Affirm. Thank people for telling about what they think or feel. Acknowledge their contributions to discussion in positive ways, even if you disagree with their ideas.

A Leader Facilitates Discussion

Ask questions. Use the questions suggested in the leader/learner helps or other questions that occurred to you as you prepared for the session. Encourage others to ask questions.

Invite silent participants to contribute ideas. If someone in the group is quiet, you might say something like: "I'm interested in what you are thinking." If they seem hesitant or shy, do not pressure them to speak. Do communicate your interest.

Gently redirect discussion when someone in the group dominates. You can do this in several ways. Remind the group as a whole that everyone's ideas are important. Invite them to respect one another and to allow others the opportunity to express their ideas. You can establish a group covenant that clarifies such respect for one another. Use structured methods such as going around the circle to allow everyone a chance to speak. Only as a last resort, speak to the person who dominates conversation after the group meeting.

13

Be willing to say, "I don't know." A leader is also a learner. You are not "teaching" a certain content to a group of "students." Instead, you are helping others and yourself to engage the great themes of the Bible as points of crossing to contemporary life and faith formation.

Introducing the Great Theme

COMMUNITY

YOU WILL BE MY WITNESSES

*C*ommunity. It is a word that evokes many different images. Think about it. What comes to mind? The senior-friendly villages in Arizona or Florida where older adults drive golf carts and gather at the "community center" to play shuffle board? Or the ex-urban wasteland where the new homes are laid out in a maze-like matrix confusing to all except those who meander the same way—day in, day out—to and from the office or school or mall?

Your neighborhood, a geographic area of perhaps three or four square blocks? your bridge club? your Bible study group? your church? your colleagues at the office or school?

They are all communities—larger or smaller networks of multi-dimensional and multi-directional relationships that in some way nurture you. If they did not, you would leave the community and go elsewhere.

You would go elsewhere because you are a social creature; you are a human being. You sense intuitively what social scientists have known for a long time: People cannot be fully human and truly happy without being in a social, covenantal relationship with others.

Some people, of course, have a limited kind of community. If they do not like their "community," it is hard for them to go elsewhere.

Homeless. When we say the word, we know what we mean and to whom we are referring. Usually, we are talking about the unshaven man sleeping in a doorway downtown with a plastic bag of possessions under his head as a pillow. We are referring to the old lady, cigarette

15

wrinkles creasing her face, wearing eight layers of clothes pushing a shopping cart full of soda cans. What we mean is that these people do not have a place to go at the end of the day where they have a bed, a dresser with clothes, and their own pictures hanging on the walls. That is home.

Yet, many of us, while not homeless ourselves, *feel* homeless—a sort of emotional homelessness. We have the bed and the dresser and the pictures; but we do not have the connection, the relationships, we want. We are in a community, but we feel homeless. We would like our relationship with spouse, family, friends, and God to improve, but we are not sure how to do that; and as a result, we feel a bit lost, homeless, and homesick for something more. We have tired of a life of *success;* we would like a life of *significance*.

Enter the Book of the Acts of the Apostles—or Acts, for short. Here is a book about the movers and shakers of the first century and how they modified their concept of home and community. For Peter, James, Barnabas, Silas, Timothy, Lydia, Priscilla, and Paul, it was not about locating one's home with a mailbox at 100 Elm Street. It was about being "at home" and in community wherever the Spirit was, wherever the opportunities were, wherever the ministry was.

This is a study about community—connectedness—and how the Holy Spirit empowered that early community to turn "the world upside down," as their critics complained (Acts 17:6).

You Will Be My Witnesses

The community formed by the Holy Spirit in Acts 2, a community of faith we refer to as "the church," was not formed to be an isolated cohort of callous and uncaring Christians with no connection to the outside world. Rather, the Spirit came expressly to empower these disciples to move beyond their comfort zones and to witness to what they had experienced.

In Acts 1:8, Jesus tells his disciples before he leaves them that "you will be my witnesses in Jerusalem, in all Judea and Samaria, and to the ends of the earth." He then disappeared from view. Moments later, "two men in white robes stood by them" and said, "Men of Galilee, why do you stand looking up toward heaven?"

In other words, their mission was not to stand around with their hands in their pockets looking into the heavens, but to get going with their arms around each other, looking at the world and all its need. Their mission, if they chose to accept it, was to be a community of witnesses, a community of testifiers, of tellers, of faith-sharing. It would be in this community of truth-tellers that they would find their authentic home.

The Fear Factor

Witnessing can be scary. No doubt about it. That is why we do not like to do it. We do not want to witness anything. We see a crime, too often, we do not come forward. We do not want to get involved. We do not want to be in court to testify. We do not want to swear to anything. We do not want to be true believers whose lives become a cliché: People who know one tune and play it all the time. We do not want to be like that. We avoid people like that. We will walk on the other side of the street to avoid people like that.

Moreover, we certainly do not want to be witnesses in the ultimate sense of the word's meaning. The Greek word is *martyria*, from which we get our word *martyr*. No thanks! We do not feel called to be martyrs. However, we are going to see in this study of Acts that this is not what Jesus meant when he said that we would be witnesses.

We are witnesses whether we like it or not. The question is, "What kind of witnesses are we?" Our lives may be saying that there is no way we can know God and be part of a caring community of believers; or our lives may suggest that we have tapped into a power, a resource, that gives us the strength and courage to live PG in an X-rated world, to live with integrity and virtue in a world of greed and consumption.

The early disciples and apostles were just like us. They were ordinary people who did not have a clue when it came to organizing, evangelizing, and theologizing. However, when the Spirit came all of a sudden, they had something to talk about; they could not stop talking, and Christians have been talking ever since. When we are finished with our study, perhaps we will be able to say with Paul, when we take a look at his farewell in the closing session, "I have fought the good fight, I have finished the race, I have kept the faith" (2 Timothy 4:6).

17

Preview

In Session 1, we will look at the coming of the Holy Spirit and how the early church worshiped, broke bread together, and reached out to their local communities and how their message spread throughout the world.

In Session 2, we will look at how the church grew through the ministry of Peter and John and how they were able to have the courage to be strong in the face of adversity.

In Session 3, we will study the example of some of the strong early leaders of the church and how they organized for maximum effectiveness. We will also discuss how the gospel went beyond familiar ethnic boundaries and how Scripture is to be encountered in the life of the community.

In Session 4, we will see how the gospel is good news for everyone, not just those who are "like us." We will also address the hard question of how to break down the biases that too often limit what God can do among us.

In Session 5, we will study the conversion of Paul and ask ourselves how God can transform lives, giving us an entirely new direction and fresh sense of purpose.

In Session 6, we will learn how the early leaders of the church worked together in different settings.

In Session 7, we will follow Paul to Ephesus and study his farewell address to the community of faith there, looking for cues that will shed light on how he had developed a sense of "home" in his ministry. We will look at how he had found in this home the support and resources he needed to be a faithful witness for Jesus Christ.

Session

1

GOD'S SPIRIT FORMS AND EMPOWERS A COMMUNITY OF FAITH

Acts 2:1-42, 47; 4:32-35

This session explores how God's life-transforming power in the Holy Spirit leads believers to live as loving, caring, sharing members of a faithful Christian community.

GATHERING

Spend a brief period greeting one another. Light a large candle on a table placed in the center of the group. This candle represents the light of God's Word, which is "a lamp to my feet and a light to my path" (Psalm 9:105). Share your name and something about your personal life, then offer two adjectives that describe who you are. Explain your adjectives. Tell why this study in the Book of Acts interests you. Pray together and thank God for the opportunities for growth we find with one another.

19

The Starbucks Principle

"How I Spent My Summer Vacation." The title of many a grade-school essay. Howard Schultz, if he were to tell the story, spent it in Italy. While he was there, he noticed something. He noticed that Italians loved to congregate at the corner coffee bar, drink espresso, and catch up on the neighborhood gossip.

It was all part of a slower way of life—this in a culture where a Catholic priest tried to ban McDonalds, because he believed that fast food threatened the very foundations of Italian, if not world, civilization.

As Schultz looked into this phenomenon closer, he realized that for Italians this corner coffee pub was one of the most significant places in the life of the Italian people. Of course, home was the most important place, the first place; and the workplace was also important, a second place.

Think about the Starbucks phenomenon. Why do people go to Starbucks? To buy a cup of coffee? Where do you go to get your "Starbucks experience"? What is in it for you? Discuss where you find connections and nurture relationships. At home? at school? at the office? What are the advantages and disadvantages of each place? Is it possible for a person to grow emotionally and spiritually if living on an island with no human contact? Are there several such places in your life that fulfill your need for connection, community, and relationships? What are they?

Schultz wondered if he could create in the United States a third place, a place that would be as fundamentally important in the life of the community as home and the office. It would be a venue where people could get away from places one and two in order to relax and interact with neighbors in place three. It would be a cozy spot to have coffee, lattes, cappuccinos, all with significant dollops of good conversation.

He went back home with this idea brewing in his mind. Today there are thousands of Starbucks in the cities and malls of America and more planned for development around the world. So here is a guy who understood our profound need for community and turned it into a multinational, multimillion-dollar operation around the world!

Where do *we* meet *our* need for community? for connectedness? for human interaction? Why do we feel a need to get out of our isolation and get into relationship? Many observers of pop culture predicted 15 years ago, as personal computing began to explode, that Americans would cocoon in a nest of convenience and solitude and never leave the house. It has not happened. Why not?

Howard Schultz was a perceptive student of the culture. He saw the need for a "third place." Could it be, however, that there is another third place? Couldn't you make the argument that the church is precisely the kind of community that Schultz had in mind except with a few add-ons such as compassion for the poor, the homeless, the disadvantaged, and a witness to the good news that God is in the world in Jesus Christ, bringing people together and drawing them to God? The beginnings of this kind of community can be traced back 2,000 years to a morning in which something spectacular happened in Jerusalem.

Waiting in the Upper Room

The story begins with 120 of the disciples closeted in an upper room in Jerusalem (Acts 1:15). Luke implies that the disciples, after the post-resurrection appearance of Jesus, had wanted to hit the road with the news of Jesus' presence. He said that "repentance and forgiveness of sins is to be proclaimed in [my] name to all nations" (Luke 24:47). Why else would he caution them to "stay . . . in the city" until the Holy Spirit comes (24:49) unless they were eager to announce to the world what they themselves had witnessed (24:48)?

In Acts 2, they are still in the upper room some 40 days after the Resurrection. We know they had been waiting in the city for almost 40 days because the Resurrection had occurred at the conclusion of the Passover feast; and it was now close to Pentecost, which occurred 40 days after Passover.

> *Acts 2 opens with the words, "When the day of Pentecost had come . . ." Look up Pentecost in Bible dictionaries or commentaries. Discuss what you discover. If there are not enough dictionaries to go around, work in teams. This activity, however, should not be done in silence. Imitate the sense of Pentecost by studying and speaking out loud as you share the results.*

Can you imagine the scene on the 39th day? Perhaps some were becoming anxious to get out, get to work, to do ministry. They were getting on one another's nerves. The coffee was cold. The take-out was getting old. Nothing was happening. They were tired of praying; they wanted to be doing something, anything.

Then Luke, the author of Acts as well as the Gospel, recorded movement. Suddenly, fire and wind appeared in a scene that invoked the image of a mountaintop Moses and the prophets of Israel riding in chariots of fire. However, there were differences. The fire was differentiated in "tongues" of flame that came to rest upon each person in the room. Clearly, the Holy Spirit had come upon them as Jesus promised; and in that moment, the church is born.

Much ink has been spilled over the meaning of the "speaking in tongues" that occurs here. The dominant view is that this is a miracle of speaking in languages that various ethnic groups could understand and not the glossolalia to which the apostle Paul refers in 1 Corinthians 12–14. People heard the good news in their own language. What implications does this fact have for hearing the good news today?

In the aftermath, a linguistic miracle or miracles occurred. They spoke to one another in "other tongues"; and those in the streets who were in town for the Feast of Pentecost heard the upper room disciples speaking to them in their native tongues. It appears there was a miracle of speaking and of hearing that day!

It is significant that the first act of the Holy Spirit upon this new community called "the church" is to empower it to speak to all the peoples of the world. The church immediately addresses the citizens of the then known world; and since that moment, the mandate of the church has been to speak the good news everywhere and at all times to everyone.

The streets of Jerusalem must have been full of commotion as it was with all the out-of-town and out-of-country guests. Add to that 120 people (Acts 1:15) speaking numerous tongues, and the confusion is exponentially multiplied. So much so that some in the crowd heard but did not understand what was going on and thought the upper room disciples were intoxicated.

Peter, the same Peter who had denied the Lord three times in the Temple precincts before the Crucifixion, now stood up boldly to set the record straight. Not only was it too early in the day for drinking, what they were witnessing was a fulfillment of the prophet Joel.

It is clear that not only had the Holy Spirit given the new church a voice to speak to the world, but that voice had fallen upon people regardless of gender or age or social rank. Sons and daughters, young men, old men, women, servants—the Holy Spirit would be poured out on all. Indeed, "Everyone who calls on the name of the Lord shall be saved" (2:21). The long and short of it is that after Peter finished preaching, about 3,000 were added to their number that day. From 120 to 3,000. One sermon!

> *As a group, read aloud Acts 2:1-21. (Consider assigning verses 8-11, where there are difficult place names to pronounce, to a volunteer.) Someone could play the role of Peter, who speaks in verses 14-21. What particularly strikes you or sparks your curiosity in this Scripture?*

Who Is the Holy Spirit?

The Holy Spirit is described as a person, not an "it." Jesus said, "I will ask the Father, and he will give you another Advocate, to be with you forever. This is the Spirit of truth, whom the world cannot receive, because it neither sees him nor knows him. You know him, because he abides with you, and he will be in you. I will not leave you orphaned; I am coming to you" (John 14:16-18).

The Holy Spirit is not the Force, as in "May the Force be with you." The Spirit of God is not an impersonal vapor or shadow. Historically, the church has considered the Holy Spirit as part of a triune Godhead. Jesus said, "All authority in heaven and on earth has been given to me. Go therefore and make disciples of all nations, baptizing them *in the name of the Father and of the Son and of the Holy Spirit,* and teaching

> *Have you ever felt the presence of the Holy Spirit in your life in an unusual way? Share the experience with others. Do you wish that you were stronger in your faith? What keeps you from sharing your faith more boldly with others?*

them to obey everything that I have commanded you. And remember, I am with you always, to the end of the age" (Matthew 28:18-20; emphasis added).

God is Father, Son, and Holy Spirit. Some prefer to think of the Trinity as God the Creator, Redeemer, and Sustainer—words that reflect the dominant personality or aspect of each person of the Trinity. Yet all the divine attributes ascribed to one of the three are present equally in the others.

A primary function of the Holy Spirit is to bear witness of Jesus Christ (John 15:26; 16:13-14). The Holy Spirit also acts as a Christian's teacher (1 Corinthians 2:9-14) who reveals God's will and God's truth to a Christian. "When the Spirit of truth comes, he will guide you into all the truth; for he will not speak on his own, but will speak whatever he hears, and he will declare to you the things that are to come" (John 16:13).

The Holy Spirit also was given to us to live within us so that we can replicate the character of God and the virtues of Jesus Christ. The evidence of this is the "fruit of the Spirit"—love, joy, peace, patience, kindness, generosity, faithfulness, gentleness, and self-control (Galatians 5:22-23). No wonder that Christians are called to walk in the Spirit (Galatians 5:25) and be filled with the Spirit (Ephesians 5:18).

What Is the Church?

> Find a partner. Together create a drawing or sculpture or write a paragraph that expresses your concept of "the ideal church." How have you experienced it? What is its purpose and mission? Tell about what you have written, sculpted, or drawn to the entire group. Display your work in a location for the entire congregation to see.

With Jesus gone, the Jesus-less disciples were alone until the Holy Spirit came on the day of Pentecost. From this moment on, the disciples were not just a ragtag group of true believers. They were a community of followers who became known as "the church."

The Greek word translated "church" is the word *ekklesia*. This word consists of a root word *kaleo*, meaning "to call," and a prefix, *ek*, meaning "from." So the church has come to be known as a group of people called out from a secular or cultural context to carry out its

24

mission in the world, to stand apart from, but in relation to the world.

The Early Life of the StarBorn Community

The church was not a Starbucks community, but you could call it a "StarBorn" community, founded as it was on Jesus Christ, the "bright morning star" (Revelation 22:16). You could describe it as a "SpiritBorn" community, brought to life, energized, and animated by the Holy Spirit on the day of Pentecost.

Yet, was this new church a true community? Was it a new "third place"?

You could argue that for the early followers of Christ the church had become a first place. Notice some of the qualities of this early expression of the church. They devoted themselves to

Read Acts 2:42-47; 4:32-35 responsively or in unison. Ask the group to be aware of how this early community of believers acted. What were their practices? What did they do? How did these things nurture them and bring them together? Discuss their sense of mission. What were they all about? How does their vision of ministry compare/contrast with that of the church today?

• **the apostles' teaching.** As new believers, these followers (not yet called "Christians") wanted and needed instruction in the faith that recognized Jesus as the Messiah. Therefore, one of the primary reasons for meeting together was to become knowledgeable about the Hebrew Scriptures and how Jesus was the fulfillment of the Scriptures. This was not a place for "tossed salad" Christianity—where everyone throws in their views and chews on it for a while. The new Christians met to learn and be taught the principles of their faith.

• **fellowship.** The time together was also an opportunity to bond with, or be comfortable with, others who shared their views.

• **the breaking of bread.** They shared a meal together; and out of this experience, a Eucharistic observance probably began. However, the meaning here is that it was in this post-Pentecostal period that the church potluck tradition emerged.

• **prayer.** Their sessions always included prayer. The content of these prayers almost certainly varied, but frequently they prayed for strength and courage in the face of cultural and political hostility (Acts 4:24-30).

These verses give us a "snapshot" of the early church. What would a snapshot of your church, your community of faith, look like? How is your church expressing itself as a loving, caring, and faithful community?

Moreover, they were together, and they had everything in common (4:32).

- They were generous: "It was distributed to each as any had need."
- They were together with glad and sincere hearts.
- They praised God.
- They enjoyed the favor of all the people.
- They shared everything they had.

If our churches are like the church described in Acts 2:42-47; 4:32-35, we probably have healthy and active churches. Is it a community most people would regard as a third place after home and the office? Is it a community that you want to be part of, that banishes any sense of spiritual "homelessness"? Is it a home you just cannot stay away from?

Perhaps this does not describe your experience. The good news is that God has promised to empower us with God's Spirit as we are open to this power. We may need to take a fresh look at our ministry. As a congregation, we may need to define what we are about and how we can take steps to be the church God wants us to be. As we make ourselves available to be channels of love and compassion for others, a SpiritBorn, energized, and mobilized community will grow and begin to reach out to others with the warmth of God's love.

CLOSING WORSHIP

Look at the hymnal your church uses. Find the section on the Holy Spirit. Choose a hymn and read or sing a verse that is meaningful to you. Close with this prayer: O God, you do not want your people to be empty, so you fill them. You fill them with your Spirit, your love, your compassion, your words, and your deeds. You do not want your people to be homeless, so you have given us each other; and you have given us your Spirit. Empower us now to share your love with those who are empty and those who are homeless, that they too might be filled and sheltered by your Spirit. Amen.

GOD'S SPIRIT HEALS AND ENCOURAGES

Acts 3:1–4:1-31

This session looks at the ministry of Peter and John in order to explore ways God's power through the Holy Spirit offers healing and courage.

GATHERING

Set up a small table or worship center with a candle and a Bible. Light the candle. Gather with the others in the group around the worship center and hold hands. Think about the following questions: Who are the differently-abled? Just those who cannot walk, hear, or see? Can we be spiritually-disabled or emotionally disabled? Tell stories about the courage of those with physical disabilities. Talk about an occasion when you have felt emotionally or spiritually disabled. Pray together, asking for the guidance of God's Spirit as you study and discuss God's gifts of healing and courage.

The Need for Healing

As human beings, we consist of body, soul, and spirit; therefore it is reasonable to assume that any one of these parts of us might at times become dysfunctional or even non-functional. Some people have experienced the loss of physical function. Others are spiritually ill, that is, they are unable to connect, or they are unresponsive to, a Power-Beyond-Themselves: God. They are limited to human resources and their own wits. So when we talk about disabilities and the need for healing, there are several levels on which this discussion can take place.

> *How would you define a miracle? How have you or the members of the group been touched by a miracle?*

Today, there is no shortage of charismatic figures who purport to carry on healing ministries. Yet their methods cast doubt upon their claims, and many so-called faith healers seem very interested in "silver and gold." You could argue that today a miracle might be met with suspicion for a number of reasons: the abuse perpetuated by charlatans, skepticism over what is real and unreal, casual use of the word itself, and technological advances and special effects that make it possible to make anything happen.

Yet our culture yearns for the miraculous. Witness the popularity of *Touched by an Angel* and *Joan of Arcadia* on television and Tony Kushner's Pulitzer prize-winning play, *Angels in America,* which was made into an epic movie event for HBO.

Tess, Monica, and Joan

A recent study by Computron Media reports that the attitudes of approximately 60 percent of Christians are influenced about heaven, God, angels, and divine intervention more strongly by television fiction than by Scripture.

A two-year study of 7,500 Christians, following a three-tiered testing process, indicates that Della Reese and Roma Downey, who portray angels in the television show *Touched by an Angel,* are more influential in shaping attitudes about God than pastors of the local congregations. A random quote from a 44-year-old pediatrician sums up another television show: "I never really understood how God works in people's lives until I started watching *Joan of Arcadia.*"[1]

People who are sensitive to those around them understand that their communities are filled with the walking wounded. "Walking wounded" is not simply a description of the physically ill. It speaks more to those who are soul-sick. That is why many churches have developed healing ministries and rituals that address physical and spiritual healing, incorporating them into the life of the church and its worship. It is clear that the physical, emotional, and spiritual well-being of people is something about which the church must be concerned when so many people champion health-care issues and healthy lifestyle choices and understand the connection between spiritual health and physical health.

Many churches are holding healing services and not just for the physically ailing. In fact, the type of healing is not specified. People who are in need of healing of any kind are encouraged to come. Discuss how the group might be part of a process to bring a healing service to the church and participate in it. What would this service look like?

Peter and John show us that to be people of God, we must be attentive to the whole person—body, soul, and spirit. In touching the body of the lame man, they reached an entire community with the news that all people have been reconciled to God through Jesus Christ, and that in him there is healing, not just of a physical complaint but of the wounds in the spirit.

Peter and John Heal a Lame Man (Acts 3:1-16)

In Acts 3:1-2, a man has no physical function in his legs. He was "a man lame from birth" (verse 2). He was not without friends, because every day "people would lay him daily at the gate of the temple called the

How have friends been a support for you during a time of stress and suffering? What qualities of these friends did you most appreciate during this time?

Beautiful Gate so that he could ask for alms from those entering the temple" (verse 2). It is always good to have friends when experiencing suffering.

No doubt, for this reason the man was well-known to those who worshiped regularly at the Temple. They knew this man. They knew he was lame; they knew he had been lame from birth. This knowledge, then, would account for their considerable astonishment when they later saw him "walking and praising God" (verse 9). It is no surprise that "they were filled with wonder and amazement at what had happened to him" (verse 10).

The man's positioning at the Temple was strategic: People were more likely to toss him change when entering or leaving worship than if they were at the market already spending money. In Judaism, giving alms, or monetary gifts, to the poor was strongly encouraged in the rabbinic tradition and Jewish writings (Tobit 4:7-11; 12:8-9). Peter and John, like all devout Jews of the day, went to the Temple to pray about 3 P.M. No doubt they had prayed earlier—at 9 A.M. and at noon that same day. Clearly, the disciples did not yet regard themselves as standing outside and apart from their Jewish faith. In their minds, they had not embraced a new religion but were still practicing Jews who had embraced Jesus as the long-awaited Messiah.

Perhaps this is the first time the lame man had actually encountered Peter and John. In any event, Luke records the first healing miracle in Acts, although others may have taken place (2:43). When the lame man asked Peter for money, he told him that he was broke and had no money to give (3:6). "I have no silver or gold, " he said, "but what I have I give you." He then commanded the man in the name of "Jesus Christ of Nazareth" to walk.

With a physician's eye, Luke describes what happens next. Peter helped the lame man to stand up, and then the man's feet and ankles became strong. He jumped to his feet and began to walk. He proceeded into the Temple court walking and leaping and praising God; and as the news spread and an astonished crowd ran to the scene of the miracle, the man clung to Peter and John while Peter addressed the crowd.

A Ministry Authenticated

The linguistic details used to describe Peter's healing and a parallel story in which Jesus healed a paralyzed man in Capernaum (Matthew 9:2-8; Mark 2:3-12; Luke 5:17-26) are similar. As in Acts, the paralyzed man was told to rise; and he jumped to his feet and went home praising God. Everyone who had seen the miracle was amazed and filled with awe (Luke 5:26). In the same way, the people who saw the beggar healed and praising God were filled with wonder and amazement (Acts 3:10). The Capernaum miracle supplied Jesus with public confirmation of his authority to forgive sins as well as to heal the sick. When the apostles healed the lame beggar at the Temple gate, they too were seen as having the same spiritual authority and power as Jesus.

Peter's marketplace sermon occurs at Solomon's Colonnade, part of the outer court of the Temple known as the Court of the Gentiles. It was a place that always was buzzing with activity. Moneychangers and merchants plied their business there, and rabbis met with their students for loud debates over the finer points of the Law. It is in this venue that Peter preached his second sermon, the first being on the day of Pentecost (2:14-36). The theme is similar: God sent Jesus whose coming the prophets predicted; but rather than receiving him, the people "handed over and rejected" him (3:13). However, God raised him from the dead; therefore there is hope if all who believe will "repent . . . and turn to God so that your sins may be wiped out" (verse 19).

This healing sets the stage for the expansion of the gospel in Jerusalem and beyond. It authenticates the ministry of Peter and John. When Peter and John spoke, people listened.

The Wimp Factor

In his book, *The Embarrassed Believer: Reviving Christian Witness in an Age of Unbelief,* Hugh Hewitt argues that Christians today are intimidated by a hostile culture and find it difficult to defend their faith.[2] Alternative relig-

What happens if we change "justify" to "to righteous"? What was Paul suggesting to his audience? What about the word reconcile? What do we mean by that word? What might it mean to people who were not part of the original "people of the covenant"?

ions, less scrutinized by the media, have stepped into the void, even though their claims might appear outlandish to many. Hewitt urges Christians to re-enter the public square without embarrassment but cautions that they must do so with intellectual vigor and honest compassion.

When it comes to sharing one's faith, many Christians suffer from the wimp factor. For some reason, it takes guts to identify openly with our faith. It is not cool to come off as a religious fanatic; and the moment you open your mouth about your Christian convictions, that is exactly what happens. You are lumped in with any number of religious wackos and weirdos. The public is not too discerning or thoughtful. It is easier to jump to quick conclusions, and most of us do not have the stomach for it.

Perhaps the problem with many Christians is that we have a hard time understanding the profound impact and difference our faith makes in our lives. Usually this is not because our faith has made no difference but rather because we have never taken the time to assess what that impact and difference is.

Peter and John Defend Their Faith (Acts 4:1-31)

Peter and John encountered a lame man, and within minutes the guy was walking and leaping and praising God. Word spread. If Peter and John had hoped to live in quiet anonymity arousing no suspicion and causing no problems, the illusion was over. Their identities as followers of Jesus were no longer secret, if it ever was. Now they would be tested for the wimp factor. Would they have the courage in the face of enormous political and religious opposition to stand strong in their faith and their convictions?

> *How do you react to the notion of Christian witness? What does it suggest to you? Do you think sharing faith is difficult? Why or why not? Explain.*

The pressure was considerable. Luke cites some of the details. Two groups were specifically identified as being upset with the uproar that Peter and John had created in the Temple precincts: the priests and the Sadducees. The latter were a politically powerful religious sect that did not believe in the resurrection of the body (Acts 4:2). These two groups accosted the two men and had with them a third person, the captain of the Temple guard (verse 1, New International Version). If you think of this happening, not on the grounds of a church or synagogue, but in the middle of the Mall of America, you get the idea. Lots of people, a lame man walking, confusion, noise, and shouting. The authorities arrested Peter and John on the spot and tossed them in jail for the night because it was too late in the day to do anything else (verse 3).

Were that to happen to us, or even were we to be threatened with such an action, we might be willing to keep quiet and go about our business. However, Peter and John were resolved. The next day, the authorities convened a hearing. Additional groups appeared: "The rulers, elders, and scribes" met in Jerusalem (verse 5). The key question was, "By what power or by what name did you do this?" (verse 7).

Perhaps response to questions is the key to witnessing and having the courage to witness. On some level, a witness answers questions. The lives of Peter and John had raised certain questions in the minds of observers. So they posed the question, and the disciples had an opportunity to answer them.

Sometimes, the question others ask is, "How can you call yourself a Christian and yet . . ." That is not the sort of question we want our lives to raise! In the case of these two apostles, the question concerned the source of their power to perform the miracle. Their response took courage, no doubt; but when witnessing is reduced to answering the questions people have about our faith, it is not so hard. It is not as if Peter and John initiated this witnessing, faith-sharing encounter. They simply responded to a question. The wimp factor was rendered moot.

Peter responded by cleverly restating the situation: He said, "Rulers of the people and elders, if we are questioned today because of a good deed done to someone who was sick and are asked how this man has been healed, let it be known to all of you, and to all the people of Israel, that this man is standing before you in good health by the name of Jesus Christ of Nazareth, whom you crucified, whom God raised from the dead" (verses 8-10). For good measure, he cited Psalms 118:22: "The stone that was rejected by you, the builders; / it has become the cornerstone" (Acts 4:11). By his response, Peter showed the growing separation between the emergent Christian community and the entrenched cultural and religious community of his day.

> *Who are the ordinary people who have been important in your journey of faith? How have they witnessed the gospel?*

However, he also did something else. He demonstrated his courage or boldness, a fact that alone astonished the observers (verse 13). Most people admire those who stand up for what they believe, if it is done in an honest and forthright way. In this case, people were genuinely amazed at Peter's boldness in what could be a life-threatening situation. They were also struck by two other factors: They noticed that Peter was an uneducated and an ordinary man.

That led them to an inescapable and undeniable conclusion: "These men had been with Jesus" (verse 13, NIV). There is no other accounting for their boldness, courage, and power with the lame man and for their articulate defense of the faith as uneducated and ordinary people. They had been with Jesus.

Peter stood in direct contrast with all the titled and educated men around him. They were the ones asking questions; Peter was the man with the formerly lame man standing beside him smiling. There is no doubt a sense in the Christian community that if the gospel is going to be spread in our communities, it is going to be advanced by a professional class of clergy, not by uneducated and ordinary people. Yet the hope of the church lies with us ordinary people.

The conclusion of the matter was reached in chambers, behind closed doors. They brought the two men before them and told them not to teach in the name of Jesus—or else. However, Peter, being bold again, asked whether it was "right in God's sight to listen to you rather than to God" (verse 19). So they threatened them again and let them go. Politically, there was no other option. People were praising God; and how can you argue against a man lame since his birth, 40 years old, who can now walk?

A Time for Boldness

For their part, Peter and John went back "to their own people" (verse 23, NIV) and gave a report. In other words, they immediately sought the refuge of their home, their community. It was in this community that they found the source of their strength and courage.

Coming together, they prayed and they asked God to help them to continue to speak with boldness (verse 29). Again, just as in the original upper room, the place where they were meeting began to rattle and roll with the power of the Holy Spirit: "They were all filled with the Holy Spirit and spoke the word of God with boldness" (verse 31).

God's Spirit gave healing. The lame man could walk. God's Spirit gave courage. The disciples' fear was anointed with boldness and courage.

CLOSING WORSHIP

Gather again around the table with the candles and the Bible. Join hands as another way to identify with the early Christian community that had to meet secretly. Pray as they prayed for boldness and courage and ask God by the Holy Spirit to bring the emotional, spiritual, and physical healing that we need. Close with the following prayer: Gracious God, thank you for empowering us differently. Thank you that our differences in ability and gifts make us stronger as a community. Thank you for offering your healing and courage to us all. Be with each of us as we go forth today and this week enabled by your strength and inspired by your presence. Amen.

[1]From The United Methodist Church General Board of Discipleship's Dan Dick's "Research Update" for April 13, 2004.

[2] From *The Embarrassed Believer: Reviving Christian Witness in an Age of Unbelief*, by Hugh Hewitt (W. Publishing Group, 1998).

Community: You Will Be My Witnesses

Session

3

STRONG CHRISTIAN LEADERS REACH OUT TO ALL PEOPLE

Acts 6:8–7:60; 8:4-40

This session looks at the ministries of Stephen and Philip in order to explore ways God calls, inspires, and guides strong leaders. It provides opportunities to identify ways we can reach out to those who may be different from us culturally or racially.

GATHERING

Light a candle and say the following prayer of illumination: "Eternal Spirit, you flow through the ages from the pages of Scripture, transforming hearts with your challenge, moving those who hear to new acts of faith, courage, and mission. Bless our hearts and minds in the study of your Word, so that we might know your presence and power more fully. We pray in the name of the Living Word. Amen."[1]

The Fox and the Hedgehog

"The fox knows many things, but the hedgehog knows one big thing." So spoke Archilochus, some 2,600 years ago. What he meant was that the fox lived a life that was complex and multiplex, a life that explored many roads and experienced many truths, a life that was as likely to diverge as converge at any given moment from the conventional wisdom. The upside is that the fox is flashy, fast, and sleek. The downside is that foxes tend to be distracted and diffused with inconsistent values and an incoherent vision.

The hedgehog is not like that at all. Jim Collins, author of the best-selling book *Good to Great,* uses the fable of the fox and the hedgehog to explain important principles of leadership. "Level 5 leaders," as Collins calls them, are people who combine strong drive or ambition with a sense of personal humility. The ambition they have is not for themselves; it is for the company or organization they lead. They are energized not by a complex set of corporate or personal goals but rather by a single unifying vision.[2]

The hedgehog is not fast, flashy, or sleek. It lives according to a single, unifying vision of the world. It knows that all it has to do is curl up into a ball, and the fox, for all of his powerful, high-flying corporate technologies, is not going to eat him up. Indeed, should he try, he will only bring calamity upon himself, slinking away with a bad taste in his mouth and a fistful of stinging spines in his gums.

Freud and the unconscious, Darwin and natural selection, Marx and class struggle, Einstein and relativity, Adam Smith and division of labor—they were all hedgehogs, according to Collins. They took a complex world and simplified it.[3]

> *What do you think are the most important qualities of leadership? You might get at this by using the letters of* leadership *in an acrostic exercise. L=Learning; E=excellence; and so on. Using a marker, write the words on a white board or a large sheet of paper.*

Stephen

What do we know about Stephen? He was probably a Greek-speaking Christian, as opposed to an Aramaic Christian. Already there were divisions in the early Church along ethnic and racial lines. Aramaic was a dialect or form of classical Hebrew spoken by most of those who became Christians after Pentecost, and it was the language Jesus spoke. Jerusalem was a cosmopolitan city, and many languages were spoken there. After Aramaic, Greek was one of the most well-known languages of the day; indeed it was the lingua franca of the cultural world at the time.

By Hebrew law, the Jews were to take care of the widows and orphans. They did not always do it, but they were supposed to. One can easily imagine that the widows and orphans of Christians were neglected. In any case, the early Christian community decided to take care of the legal responsibility themselves and not to rely on Temple alms to take care of them. Complaints soon arose that the Greek-speaking widows and orphans were being neglected. The apostles appointed deacons to handle this; and it is likely, if not astonishing, that the seven deacons they appointed were all Greek-speakers (they appear to have Greek names), and Stephen was one of them.

The qualifications were explicit: They were to be people "of good standing, full of the Spirit and of wisdom" (Acts 6:3). Stephen evidently stood out as a potential candidate because he was placed at the top of the list, and he alone was identified as someone who was "a man full of faith and the Holy Spirit" (verse 5). His curriculum vitae might have read differently were he a "foxy" leader in our contemporary culture: administrative skills, knowledge of computer software, and bi- or trilingual. The most crucial qualification of this Level 5 leader was that he had a tank of faith that was running on full. He was also high on the Holy Spirit. No wonder that as his accusers watched him they thought "that his face was like the face of an angel" (verse 15).

> *Read Acts 6. What traits of leadership do you see in the Scripture? Why do you think those who argued with Stephen made false accusations against him? What situations in the contemporary world seem similar to the conflict described in verses 9-15? How do you think Stephen's qualities of leadership affected the situation?*

The Sermon and the Stoning

> *What news stories or situations in your community or local church demonstrate our unkindness to those who hold up the mirror, who suggest an alternative course, or who shatter cultural and religious taboos?*

Unlike the hedgehog of the fable, this valiant leader suffers and pays the ultimate price for being a truth-teller. It happens a lot these days. We do not treat kindly those who hold up the mirror, who suggest an alternative course, or who shatter cultural and religious taboos.

The religious and theological agenda, together with its practical implications for daily religious and cultural life, were as radical as anything we might want to discuss today that is dividing our culture. What Stephen appeared to be suggesting was the negation of millenniums of religious history and customs, which would have been all the more startling in an oral culture where change occurs slowly.

Moreover, as Rex Miller notes in his book *The Millennium Matrix*, in an oral culture, the message is inextricably linked to the messenger.[4] It was not until the invention of the printing press that people were able to separate the news from the channel of the news. The prophet foretells a dark future? Kill the prophet. The messenger is the bearer of bad news? Kill the messenger. (See David's application of this principle in 2 Samuel 4:9-11.)

It happens again in the story of Stephen. People were recruited to tell lies about the message. The lies concerned what Stephen allegedly said about Moses and about God. Stephen preached a powerful sermon. At first glance, like Peter's sermon, it appears to be a summary of Jewish history. Unlike Peter, however, Stephen did not quote Scripture or try to explain it. Also unlike Peter, Stephen did not mention Jesus until he was almost finished. Even then, he referred to Jesus as "the Righteous One" (Acts 7:52).

> *Read Stephen's sermon in Acts 7:1-43. What do you think Stephen was trying to say when he mentioned Abraham, Joseph, and Moses?*

The sermon deals first with Abraham, then Joseph, and then Moses. It also deals with God and where God dwells. God spoke to and appeared to

Abraham before he lived in Haran—that is, while he lived in Mesopotamia, where much of present-day Iraq is located. Jewish tradition understood that God spoke to Abraham at Haran but not before. Even when Abraham was in Canaan, he considered himself a pilgrim, not linked to latitude and longitude. The point is that God is not limited to geographical boundaries. Joseph was abused and rejected by his own brothers. Moses, too, was rejected by his own people and lived in the wilderness for 40 years. Even after the Exodus, he was once again rejected by his own people.

> *Read Acts 7:44-54. Why do you think those who heard Stephen "became enraged and ground their teeth at Stephen"?*

God was said to live in the Tabernacle, which was a portable temple. Then the Israelites received a shining, gleaming new Temple. It was glorious, but was God there? God was with the people in the humble wilderness tent; but God did not dwell in this temple, Stephen said. With a vision of the one true thing, Stephen seemed to point to a time when the Temple would cease to be the center of the cultural and religious life of the people. He saw his people on the cusp of a great revolution, and he invited his friends and enemies to join him.

The "hedgehog concept" in this case: God is bigger than our human boundaries, and sometimes we reject those who proclaim this vision. The religious leaders who listened to Stephen's message refused it. They killed the messenger.

Martyr? Who Me?

We have met people with a martyr complex. Life is a burden. Everything seems to wear them down. God forbid that they should have to shoulder one more responsibility; but if they are asked, they will—gladly—(sigh!) do it.

"You go now, and have a good time with your friends," the widowed mother says to her adult son. "I'll be fine . . . here in this house . . . alone . . . in the

> *Discuss the natural tendency to mistreat those who challenge our assumptions. Can you think of modern-day examples? Nelson Mandela, Martin Luther King Jr., Yitzhak Rabin, Anwar Sadat, Veronica Guerin come to mind. Why do we react this way to the messenger?*

dark . . . by myself. Go on, have a good time. I'm sure that nothing will happen. It's been three years since the last stroke . . . when you left before."

These are not the kind of leaders we want, nor are they the kind of leaders who are useful to any organization or movement. Certainly, those in the early church did not feel that suffering was beyond their job description. They knew that change is painful and that it can hurt.

The word *martyr* comes from the Greek word *martyria*, meaning "to witness." A *marturion* was a testimony, an act by which one confirmed something by referring to one's own experience. Today, the word has come to refer to those who choose to suffer death rather than renounce religious principles, or to those who make great sacrifices or suffer much in order to further a belief, cause, or principle. However, the root meaning of the word refers simply to making a witness, statement, or testimony about one's experience. Such a person was a martyr.

> *How do you define a* martyr? *What feelings or thoughts come to you when you think about martyrdom in Christian tradition? in the contemporary world?*

Stephen did not seek his martyrdom. Instead, his death was like the death of Jesus, who wondered if it was possible to avoid crucifixion: "Father, if it is possible, may this cup be taken from me" (Matthew 26:39, NIV). However, as strange as it may sound, early church leaders had to caution people from seeking their death, including those who pled with the executioner to lop of their heads for the sake of Christ.

A new era of martyrdom seems to have dawned on us in this millennium. Innocent people are being beheaded in the Middle East. Extremists in the Islamic religion strap bombs on themselves and detonate them in crowded restaurants and buses. Yet is this kind of self-martyrdom the same thing as the death of someone who, not seeking death, suffers for the sake of an idea? Here in America, such physical suffering is not likely to occur; but we often are not kind to our leaders who stand at the front lines of the religious and cultural wars pointing people to God's way. Perhaps Stephen's witness can still be instructive to us today.

The Samaritans and Philip (Acts 8:4-25)

On the sidelines and in the shadows was an extraordinary figure who aided and abetted the execution of Stephen with his silence and by being the custodian of the clothes the attackers cast off in order to hurl their rocks and stones better (Acts 7:58). Saul, who would later be known to the church and the world as the apostle Paul, "approved of their killing him" (8:1). He went on to become a de facto head of homeland religious security by "ravaging the church by entering house after house; dragging off both men and women, he committed them to prison" (verse 3).

Stephen's assassination seems to have touched off a riot or at least inflamed the passions of anti-Christian sentiment in Jerusalem (although they were not yet called "Christians"), because that very day "a severe persecution began against the church" (verse 1). The effect was to send Christ-followers fleeing for their lives beyond Jerusalem, to Samaria, and to other parts of the then-known world. The ripple effect of that action was that wherever they went when thus scattered, they talked about the Messiah; and small but influential congregations would spring up everywhere.

The first of such localities beyond Jerusalem was Samaria. It is in Samaria that we see a new leader of the church emerge: Philip, also known in church tradition as Philip the evangelist. Philip was a remarkable leader because he "got it" even before the apostle Peter did. Philip, perhaps intuitively, understood that the good news was not for Israel alone, but for all people. Peter needed a vision during an afternoon nap in Joppa before he got the big picture, before he understood the hedgehog "one, true thing" (10:9-16).

For centuries, Samaria was culturally off limits for Jews. However, Philip went to Samaria, preached, performed "signs and wonders," and had spectacular success. He even converted the local shaman who was something of a cult figure, and there may have been a series of

> *Read Acts 8:9-21. How do you think Philip and Peter would respond to contemporary televangelists who consistently ask for money? How do you interpret "God's gift" in Acts 8:14-21? What connections do you see between God's gift and leadership?*

one-upmanship as Simon and Philip outdid each other with their miracles. However, Simon became a convert for reasons that may have
been related to the power that Philip demonstrated.

Simon, sometimes called "the sorcerer," later asked Peter to lay
hands on him so that he might have the same power. He even offered
him money to do so. Peter responded with integrity; and quite unlike
many so-called faith healers today, he said, "May your silver perish with
you, because you thought you could obtain God's gift with money!"
(8:20).

Seismic Change Shatters Barriers

One cannot overstate the upheaval that merely preaching Jesus as
the Messiah caused for the Jews or that preaching Jesus as the Messiah
to Gentiles caused for new Jewish Christians. The upheaval was seis-
mic. Prejudices abounded and were deeply rooted and engrained in
millenniums of cultural and religious history. However, Philip saw that
a new day had dawned.

Today, perhaps we are still looking at the sunset of an old day and
not the sunrise of the new. According to Edward Gilbreath, in the
1950s, *Reader's Digest* quoted the Reverend Billy Graham as having
said that the "most segregated hour in America is on Sunday morning
at 11 A.M."[5] Graham's observation is still true. Most adults tend to connect with people of their own "tribe and nation."

Yet prejudice is not confined to ethnic groups; it exists wherever and
whenever we come in contact with those who are different from ourselves. These views—of men about women, women about men,
Southerners about Northerners, Northerners about Southerners, gays
about straights, straights about gays, singles about marrieds, marrieds
about singles, the young about the aged, the aged about the young, the
Republicans about the Democrats, the Democrats about the
Republicans, the rich about the poor,
the poor about the rich, job-holders
about the jobless, the jobless about
job-holders, smokers about non-
smokers, non-smokers about smokers,
Americans about Muslims, Muslims

> *What evidence do you see
> in your community that
> the river of religious, polit-
> ical, and ethnic prejudice
> still runs deep?*

44

about Americans, the abled about the differently-abled, the differently-abled about the abled, those who have about those who have not, those who have not about those who have—all embody a set of biases that we willingly seem to reinforce. Have I missed anyone here? We need leaders who hold up the mirror and who are willing even to suffer to do so. Stephen and Philip were such leaders.

The Ethiopian Official (Acts 8:26-40)

Another example quickly unfolds involving Philip, an example that demonstrates again his utter willingness to abandon tradition in favor of a new—and utterly unheard of—path. Philip was instructed and divinely transported to Gaza by way of a desert road where, fortuitously, he encountered an Ethiopian on his way home to the upper region of the Nile.

Here was a man who was starkly "other" in many ways. He was an Ethiopian, of another land and culture. He was a eunuch and thus of a class whose access to religious privilege was severely limited by Jewish ritual law. He was educated; he could read Scripture, even if he could not understand it.

Evidently, the man had stopped at a roadside rest stop and was reading Scripture in his idling chariot. Philip approached and heard the man reading aloud from Isaiah, from one of the servant songs (Isaiah 53:7-8), that the early church came to understand as a foreshadowing of Jesus, the Messiah. Philip engaged the man in conversation; and he, in turn, asked Philip if he knew to whom this text was referring. It was all the opening Philip needed.

> *Read Acts 8:26-40 and Isaiah 53:7-8. What do these passages say to you about breaking religious and social barriers? In what ways can your local church reach through social, ethnic, or cultural barriers to reach others with the good news of God's love?*

Self-help Does Not Always Help

We live in a do-it-yourself culture, one in which were it not for self-help books, bookstores would be out of business. In this case, self-help clearly had its limits. This official needed help, tried to get it himself, and could not do it without community. Yet, before he met Philip, he was alienated from the religious community because of social and religious barriers.

> *In what ways can individuals "check and balance" independent study of Scripture or individual religious experience with Christian tradition and community? What value do you see in such checks and balances?*

He needed the help of the emerging Christian community, which Philip represented, to apply Scripture. Acts 8:26-40 underscores again that private, individual study of Scripture, while valuable, should be checked and balanced against the informed study of tradition and community.

It is also important to note that while the man had many of the advantages of a privileged life in the court of royalty, he appears to have needed and wanted more. Scripture is the starting point for discovering what God wants of us and desires to give to us. Philip kept it simple. He did not get into heavy theological or psychological discussions with the official. He simply "proclaimed to him the good news about Jesus" (verse 35).

Spirit-filled Leaders

To return to our opening image, Stephen and Philip demonstrated hedgehog leadership because they offered one simple truth: the power and love of God through Jesus Christ. They were Spirit-filled leaders who stood within a community and fearlessly pronounced the good news without regard to personal safety or public perception. Both men represent the type of leaders we need today.

CLOSING WORSHIP

Say aloud the name or names of people who have been instrumental in your faith formation or who have been inspirational examples for your life. Then offer the following prayer of gratitude for those who have been or still are our leaders: God, thank you for giving us people in our history who have been lights in our darkness. Forgive us when we have fought against the light, attempting to extinguish it. Thank you for the leaders who influence us still. Give us the grace and wisdom to lead others. Amen.

[1]From "Worship Resources," *www.HomileticsOnline.com.* Used by permission of Communication Resources, Inc.

[2]From *Good to Great: Why Some Companies Make the Leap . . . and Others Do Not,* by Jim Collins (HarperBusiness, 2001).

[3]*Good to Great;* page 90.

[4]From *The Millennium Matrix,* by Rex Miller (Jossey-Bass, 2004); page 27.

[5]From "Billy Graham, the Unifier," in *Christianity Today* at *http://ctlibrary.com/7879.*

Community: You Will Be My Witnesses

Session

4

GOD'S SPIRIT EMPOWERS US TO OVERCOME RELIGIOUS PREJUDICES

Acts 1:1-48; 12:1-17

This session looks at Peter's ministry to explore ways to overcome our own religious prejudices and to persevere in the face of such prejudice from others.

GATHERING

Light a candle. Take a few moments silently to consider how religious prejudice exists in your community. What changes need to take place in your community and within your life? Then pray the following prayer for guidance: O heavenly God, your word is our source of light, enlightening our paths, erasing our blindness. In our study, shrine your truth. Speak to us boldly once again, that we may proclaim your truth with courage.

A "Smart" World

What are some other examples of "smart" or "intelligent" objects? What do such objects say to you about our culture? How do you feel about such objects? Who has access to such objects? Who does not?

No one likes to be thought of as stupid, thus the wild success of books written for "idiots" and "dummies." It also accounts for the trillion dollar-industry in smart chips—programmable microchip sensors that make common, ordinary objects intelligent. Today we have "smart" credit cards, TVs, VCRs, DVDs, Palm Pilots, cars, refrigerators, microwaves, energy systems, and cameras. Water bottles let us know when the contents need to be cooled; bookshelves complain when they are dangerously overloaded. Putting together a desk? Green sensors will light up when you have correctly inserted Panel A into Slot A, while a red light will flash if you are assembling a piece incorrectly. Consider keys. Now we can lock, unlock, set alarms, and more remotely with our smart keys. Jesus was very much in on this "smart" movement! That is why he wanted Peter, one of his lead disciples, to be smart. He gave Peter the "keys to the kingdom" (Matthew 16:19).

Peter's Smart Keys

Peter used the "smart keys," the keys to the kingdom, at least twice. The first time, he used them to unlock the kingdom of God to the Jewish community by preaching that Jesus who was crucified was the long-awaited Messiah (Acts 2). The Jewish community responded in amazing numbers. The second time, Peter used the keys to unlock the kingdom to the Gentiles, a non-Jewish audience. However, it took some persuading to get Peter to unlock the house to visitors who had hitherto been unwelcome.

Read Acts 10. What in this Scripture challenges you or makes you want to know more? What connections do you make with the image of "smart" keys to the kingdom?

Acts 10 tells the story of how Peter changed his thinking and abandoned his prejudices. The story begins with two visions: that of Cornelius, a soldier, and that of Peter, a fisherman.

First the Soldier

His name was Cornelius. He was a Gentile and a centurion, which meant he was in command of a regiment of 100 men known as the Italian Regiment (10:1, NIV).

Cornelius was a "God-fearer." This term was used to describe those Gentiles who worshiped God and perhaps even observed many Jewish rituals and customs but were not circumcised and thus were not full participants in the community. While he was devout and generous and prayed to God on a regular basis (verse 2), Cornelius had not converted to Judaism; and any casual or social association with Cornelius by a Jew would have been problematic.

God visited Cornelius in a vision. An angel of God told him that his faith and good works had not gone unnoticed. He was told to send for Simon (Peter) who was staying with another Simon, a tanner by trade, in Joppa just down the road. Cornelius immediately began preparations to send the men. By noon of the following day, they were on the road, approaching the city of Joppa.

Are there people in your community of faith who worship regularly but who have not become members or have not become active in the ministries of the church? Who are they? What are their gifts? Why do they attend? What do they like about your congregation? What ministries or groups in your church might appeal to them?

Now, the Fisherman

Cut now to Joppa and the house of Simon the tanner. Unaware that Cornelius's party was on its way to fetch him, men perhaps from the Italian Regiment, Peter went to the roof of the house to pray. While there, he became hungry; and his hosts prepared something for him to eat. During the preparations, Peter "fell into a trance" (verse 10).

Keep in mind that Peter had already been somewhat prepared for what was about to happen. Their ethnic and religious mixture evoked severe prejudices, giving power, therefore, to Jesus' story of the good Samaritan (Luke 10:25-27). Peter went to Samaria to check it out (Acts 8:14-25). There, he prayed with the new Samaritan believers; and they, too, received the Holy Spirit, as had Jewish believers in Jerusalem on the day of Pentecost (Chapter 2).

Peter was also staying at the house of Simon, who had a great ocean view and ocean-front property; but Simon's occupation as a tanner meant that he made leather and thus handled and touched dead animals. It was a profession that by definition rendered him unclean, and off limits to a Law-observing Jew who would be required to stay away from an unclean person. However,

> *Talk about recent paradigm shifts and ones not so recent (for example, the shift from an oral to a print to a broadcast culture; the shift in ethnic perceptions since 1954; the changes introduced by television, the interstate highway system, and the Internet). How did these and other changes affect the way we think about the world? about others? about the future? about lifestyle? about faith?*

Simon was no doubt a Jewish believer; and Peter had no qualms about accepting his hospitality. Thus prepared, Peter began to pray on the housetop with the ocean in view, the breezes cooling his body, the salt air filling his lungs, and someone down below preparing him a noon meal. Things became interesting as God attempted to smart-size Peter and convinced him to use his keys to open yet another door that had been locked by millenniums of religious law and custom. Peter was about to experience a paradigm shift.

Peter Dreamed He Was in Food Court Heaven

It is not that there was no precedent for Gentiles believing God and becoming full participants in the community of faith. Rahab the prostitute of Jericho (Joshua 2) saved the Israelite spies when she recognized them as God's servants. She would become an ancestor of Jesus Christ (Matthew 1:5). Ruth the Moabite was introduced to Israel's God through her mother-in-law, Naomi. She would become the great-grandmother of David and thus an ancestor of Jesus as well. In both cases and in others, Gentiles came to God through a realignment of their religious practices with Judaism.

The question as yet unanswered for Peter was whether he could offer the good news of salvation through Christ without adding the requirement that the Gentiles become practicing Jews. Peter dozed while lunch was being prepared. He saw a large sheet descending from heaven in which—bizarrely—were all sorts of animals, a mixture of "clean and unclean" animals, designations based on whether Jews were allowed to eat them. A voice said, "Get up, Peter; kill and eat" (Acts 10:13). Peter, even in his dreams, refused to partake of the animals he perceived as being unclean. It was morally impossible for him to consciously or unconsciously violate his religious upbringing: "By no means, Lord; for I have never eaten anything that is profane or unclean" (verse 14).

What God said to Peter next was the "smart key" of the door that Peter himself would open: "What God has made clean, you must not call profane" (verse 15). This verbal exchange in the vision occurred three times. As Peter awoke, three emissaries from the house of Cornelius arrived and inquired loudly as to the whereabouts of "Simon, who was called Peter" (verse 18). The Spirit prodded Peter and told him to go with the men who were downstairs.

Peter had the smart keys. He had a feeling that God wanted him to use them again. He greeted the men and invited them to stay and be his guests (verse 23). These were baby steps. An orthodox Jew would have invited the men to step out into the street or find lodging elsewhere in the city. Peter did not completely "get it" at this point, but he was beginning to "get it."

The account of Luke here continues by describing how Peter journeyed to Caesarea to visit Cornelius the next day. Luke records their cordial meeting and Peter's subsequent oration in which he acknowledged that his behavior, for a Jew, had been unusual: "You yourselves know that it is unlawful for a Jew to associate with or to visit a Gentile; but God has shown me that I should not call anyone profane or unclean" (verse 28). Again, Peter preached to an audience quite unlike the one he or Stephen faced in Jerusalem.

The fact that Luke gave so much attention to this story is significant. We read accounts of Cornelius's vision, of Peter's vision, of Cornelius's testimony after Peter's arrival, and of Peter's sermon. In Chapter 11,

Peter goes over it all again for the benefit of believers in Jerusalem. Luke's rationale here is to ensure that there is no mistaking of the meaning of what happened. He also wanted to emphasize the nature of the religious earthquake that was about to shake the fledging new community along fault lines that were centuries deep and millennia wide.

God Does Not Play Favorites

The thematic statement of Peter's sermon comes early: "I truly understand that God shows no partiality" (verse 34). The NIV translates "partiality" as "favoritism." Either of these two words is probably easier to connect with than "prejudice."

What paradigm was in operation prior to Peter's vision on the rooftop? What happens when we believe that God is leading us to take a stand against the cultural and political norms? Discuss situations in the past where leaders broke with tradition and went against prevailing and popular opinion and eventually won the day or at least began to change attitudes. How can we know when it is okay to break the rules in order to further a cause we believe to be just?

Peter had inserted the key, turned it, and not only opened the door, but blew it off its hinges. Peter was no dummy. He had been smart-sized and Spirit-chipped to understand that God was doing a new thing. God was doing what God does. God shows no prejudice. God does not play favorites. Period.

While Israel's self-perception was that it had "most-favored status" with God, that they were, in fact, the "chosen people," this belief led them to misunderstand God's intentions. Israel was to be the nation through which God could manifest the "wideness of God's mercy," his utter, eternal, all-encompassing love to all people. While we are loathe to admit we harbor prejudices—and it is no sure thing that we do not—it is harder to say that we do not have favorites or play favorites.

What experiences have you had with favoritism? What was the effect of the favoritism? How did it affect relationships? friendships? family life? church community?

Peter in Prison (Acts 12:1-17)

Persecution had broken out when Stephen was stoned to death. As word spread that this new belief system was opening its doors to the Gentiles, the entire community was in an uproar. King Herod Agrippa I was a people-pleasing politician of the first order. Wanting to keep the peace and to please the Jewish leadership, he was determined to take a hard line approach.

He had James, the brother of John, arrested and then promptly executed him (12:2). When the polls showed widespread support for his actions, Herod arrested Peter and threw him in prison.

Were it not for the Jewish Feast of the Unleavened Bread, King Herod no doubt would have taken the sword to him. The Feast of the Unleavened Bread and Passover were two distinct observances; but the former followed the latter sequentially, and the two feasts were often thought of, or spoken of, as one and the same. Jesus was executed during Passover, but Herod deferred Peter's execution.[1]

Peter was thrown in prison where he was placed under the guard of 16 soldiers who could cover the four three-hour watches with four guards stationed during each watch. Peter spent the night sleeping between two guards and chained to both. Little did these soldiers know that within 24 hours, all of them would be dead; and Peter would be alive and well, his whereabouts unknown (verses 18-19).

Peter was sleeping when an angel appeared and awakened him, telling him to get dressed: "Fasten your belt and put on your sandals. . . . Wrap your cloak around you and follow me" (verse 8). Peter did as the angel commanded. Peter was not fully conscious; he sleepwalked past two contingents of guards and through the iron gate to the city. Once past the gates of the city, the angel disappeared; and Peter came to his senses.

Realizing that he was free and on the loose, a fugitive from the law, Peter ran to the nearest safe house, which was the home of Mary, the mother of John Mark. Unknown to him, a prayer meeting "where many had gathered" (verse 12) had convened in Mary's house. There were people who had been praying specifically for Peter's release while he languished in jail and while he and the angel of the Lord had been making their way through the city.

Luke's account of his appearance at Mary's home has all the touches of a great storyteller. A servant girl, Rhoda, answered the knock at the outer gate (verse 13) and recognized Peter's voice, perhaps before she had even made it to the gate. Rather than rushing to the

> *Why do you think Peter's Christian friends were so surprised at Peter's deliverance from religious persecution?*

gate to let Peter in, Rhoda left him standing in the darkness and rushed back to the prayer meeting to announce that the object of their prayers was standing at the outer gate!

Those who were praying for Peter's release told Rhoda that she was crazy, casting doubt on the depth of their faith as they prayed. As the conversation continued, Rhoda stuck to her story, so the group concluded that it must be his angel, that it was Peter's guardian angel—in keeping with the widely held view that the moment a person dies, his guardian angel appears. To take this view then was to assume that Peter had been executed in prison and that their prayers had not been answered as they had hoped.

Ignored at the gate, Peter continued to knock. The people finally opened the gate, suggesting that Rhoda's persistence and the continual knocking had motivated them to leave their prayer meeting to see what the commotion was about. Of course, Peter was standing there. God had delivered him from persecution instigated by religious prejudice. Peter had to motion "to them with his hand to be silent" (verse 17), and then he told how his release occurred. Evidently he did not stay long, for after these remarks, Luke says that "[Peter] left and went to another place" (verse 17).

> *Read Acts 12:1-17. With the entire group, act out the scene in this story of Peter's deliverance. Imagine yourselves inside Mary's house. You are praying. Designate one of the group to be Rhoda and another to be Peter. Conclude the scene with the group gathered at the door, with Peter explaining what happened. Then return to your seats and discuss what you might be praying for today.*

Getting Smart

It would be cool if we could take a smart pill, like those on the market today, that would erase the harmful prejudices and biases that generate a sectarian spirit among us. Perhaps the first smart thing to do would be to follow the example of the Christians who met at Mary's house to pray. We might begin to pray for ourselves that we would understand that God is a God who is always creating and doing something new. We may not like it, but we had better get used to it. We might also pray for ourselves that we would understand and see what this new thing is in our church and world today, and that we would remember that there are Christians who suffer for their faith in the Sudan, India, and elsewhere. We should also recall that people of other faiths and political persuasions suffer for the ideas they espouse.

It is a mark of the growing sense of community in the early church that believers were meeting to pray for one another. That they could not believe that their prayers were answered is a sign that their faith, perhaps like ours, needed to grow.

When we as a community of faith gather to pray for those who need our support, we might remember that there are many who are imprisoned but not in a prison of bricks and mortar. Their prison is one of the soul and the spirit. Some face the oppression of depression. Some are locked into a downward spiral of addiction and dependency. Others feel trapped in a job or a dead marriage and do not know how to escape the one or heal the other. Some are caught in a web of deceit and fraud. Others live in fear of domestic violence and do not know how to find freedom. Such souls need our prayers, not our prejudice. They need our blessings, not our biases.

Peter took the keys to the kingdom and opened the doors first to his countrymen and then a second time to the Gentiles, that is, to all of God's children. He taught us that God plays no favorites, and his example is an invitation for us to walk through the doors that have been opened to us. To do so as a supporting, prayerful community that remembers that what God has called clean we should not call unclean.

It is a smart way—the only way—to walk in our pilgrim journey.

CLOSING WORSHIP

Create a "smart key" to God's kingdom from poster paper. Cut it out. Write something on your key that you could do in the week ahead to break the barriers of religious prejudice and to open the doors of your church to others who may feel excluded or persecuted. Place your key where you will see it daily. Pray about your smart key.

Close by praying the Lord's Prayer aloud.

[1]From "The Acts of the Apostles," by Johannes Munck in *The Anchor Bible* (Doubleday, 1967); page 113.

Session 5

GOD'S SPIRIT TRANSFORMS LIVES

Acts 9:1-31

This session looks at the way God transforms the life of Paul in order to identify ways God transforms our lives as we choose to follow Christ

GATHERING

Light a candle. Before prayer, have a brief discussion about the makeover shows on television. If you were to be ambushed for a makeover, what would be done to you or to your house? Consider ways that God is in the makeover business. Pray conversationally as a group by offering prayer sentences, one person at a time, as God's Spirit moves you to do so. When all have had opportunity to offer a sentence or to pray silently, close the prayer time with "Amen."

Extreme Makeover

You have seen them on television: makeover shows in which a fashion-impaired man or woman is ambushed by a fashion crew from some show (for example, *Oprah*). Within hours, they are transformed into something gorgeous.

One show in particular is *What Not to Wear,* a program that began in the United Kingdom. A US version has also been made. The hosts of the show are two thirty-something women, Trinny Woodall and Susannah Constantine, who are brutally frank when assessing the frumpy outfits and mismatched shirts and trousers people are wearing these days.

Granted, Trinny and Susannah are equally as frank about their own wardrobes: "Trousers were invented to cover my thick ankles," says Trinny. Susannah confesses freely that she's "got a flaccid stomach . . . and chins that are breeding."[1]

More than a dozen such makeover shows dot the television land-scape. What they are making over ranges from wardrobes to hairstyles to homes to gardens to physical anatomy—all made possible with new gadgets, mousse, and silicon.

Most of us are no doubt relatively satisfied with what we have in our closets and in our homes and with what our hair or our bodies look like. If we are not happy, we are really not ready to make any radical changes. Even if we are open to making some changes, many people do not give a second thought to the possible need for an inner—not outer—transformation.

> *What in your life would benefit from an extreme makeover?*
> *Your wardrobe? house? hair? other?*

Saul Got a Makeover

Saul, in our text, is about to get an extreme makeover; but he does not know it. We met Saul, you remember, as one of the bystanders at the murder of Stephen, a deacon in the early Christian community in Jerusalem. Saul stood by watching and holding the cloaks and togas of those who were part of the mob stoning the outspoken witness to the faith (Acts 7:58; 8:1).

Saul shifted from bystander to terminator quickly. He became one of the most feared religious terrorists of his time: "Saul was ravaging the church by entering house after house; dragging off both men and women, he committed them to prison" (8:3). In Chapter 9, it is clear that Saul's zeal had not abated: "Meanwhile Saul, still breathing threats and murder against the disciples of the Lord, went to the high priest" (verse 1). He later recalled that he "was violently persecuting the church of God and was trying to destroy it" (Galatians 1:13).

The Christian community had been growing. It was moving south. Witness Philip's incursion into Gaza in Acts 8. However, the Christian community was also growing north beyond Jerusalem into Samaria (8:4-25) and evidently even as far north as Damascus of Syria.

The community was known as "the Way" (9:2), and the whole thing was getting way out of hand as far as Saul was concerned. He turned his attention from the Christians in Jerusalem to these new Christians in Damascus and sought permission from authorities to go after them. Getting his marching orders, Saul left for Damascus, setting the stage for one of the most dramatic conversion stories in all of literature— religious or otherwise. Verses 1-31 tell of Saul's makeover ambush on the road to Damascus, when Saul least expected it. It occurs two more times in 22:1-29 and again in 26:1-32, which demonstrates the importance of the ministry of the one, single person who more than anyone else was responsible for bringing the gospel to the Gentiles: Paul. Clearly, Luke understood that this makeover event was a watershed moment in the history of the church.

Read Acts 9:1-31; 22:1-29; 26:1-32. What particularly interests you in these three Scriptures? What questions do the Scriptures bring to your mind? List the changes you see in Saul as the result of his extreme makeover? Discuss your list with another person in the group.

Who Was Saul?

Much of what we know of Saul comes from his own statements. He was "born a [Roman] citizen" (22:28) in Tarsus of Cilicia of Jewish parents; he was immediately circumcised and raised in Jerusalem. Saul received the equivalent of a Harvard education when he studied with the great master, Gamaliel, a Pharisee (Acts 22:3; 23:6; Philippians 3:5). In his own words, he admits that "I advanced in Judaism beyond many among my people of the same age, for I was far more zealous for the traditions of my ancestors" (Galatians 1:14). When Saul committed himself to a cause, he did so with incredible energy. When he persecuted the church, he did so because he must have believed that the followers of the Way not only represented a danger to the established traditions of Judaism but that they were also wrong in the claims they made about Jesus. No wonder he "was convinced that [he] ought to do many things against the name of Jesus of Nazareth" (Acts 26:9).

Christians claimed that Jesus was the Son of God—a blasphemous notion to any monotheistic Jew—and that he was the Christ, a claim authenticated by their assertion of the Resurrection. As a Pharisee, Saul believed in the resurrection; but he did not believe that Jesus had been resurrected. Granted, it would have been easy to dispel any notion that Jesus was dead if Saul and the authorities in Jerusalem had been able to produce a body; but conventional wisdom held that the disciples had stolen the body. Saul believed that the followers of Jesus were not only dangerous, but they were deceptive.

Saul, then, was committed to a cause. He could not know that he was wrong, that he was in need of a transformation, that he would himself utterly convert, turn around, and embrace the beliefs that were anathema to him. He may have been pulled toward his conversion without even knowing it. He is described by Jesus as someone who was kicking "against the goads" (verse 14), an old Gentile proverb. As he watched Stephen die, Saul must have felt a sense of unease or of doubt. He saw how articulate Stephen was in his defense of his faith. That must have appealed to Saul's intellectual curiosity. He must have been impressed with Stephen's courage in the face of danger, even death. He must have recalled that before Stephen died he said, "I see the heavens opened and the Son of Man standing at the right hand of God!" (7:56). Why would

> *Read Acts 7:54–8:1. What do you think might have been going through Saul's mind and heart as he witnessed the stoning of Stephen?*

> *Talk about experiences in which the blind spots were suddenly removed and you saw yourself as others, or perhaps God, saw you. What was good about you that you had not previously acknowledged? What, if anything, needed to be changed? How hard was it to change?*

Stephen lie about something like that?

From Terminator to Transformer

It is not easy to see our own need for a makeover. Why is that? It is easy enough to see what other people need to do to get their act together, to get a life, to get a new life. However, assessing our own need for change and transformation is virtually impossible. That is why we often need a community—a family, network of friends, loved ones—to help us. Yet, even then, we are likely to resist opening up to change.

How many really want to visit a counselor when their marriages are on the rocks? How hard is it to kick a habit that is injurious to one's health? How easy is it not to read a book and watch TV instead? How hard is it to commit to regular worship attendance because it feeds our souls? How hard is it to commit to 30 minutes of exercise three times a week?

Hard. Really tough. Again, why is it so hard to see our own needs? We might be wearing a blindfold. We simply cannot see.

In this case, God got hold of Saul, knowing that he was ready and prepared to be a transformer rather than a terminator, and completely turned him around in a new direction. Saul had several blindfolds in place: the blindfold of rigid traditionalism; the blindfold of intellectual dogmatism; and the blindfold of nationalism.

Our masks might be different. Pride often stands in the way. Stubborn refusal to change is a problem. Then there is the convoluted argument that people should accept us the way we are. It is the Popeye Protocol: "I yam what I yam."

Saul Hit the Road

Saul, armed with his documents, set out for Damascus. He had almost arrived when "suddenly a light from heaven flashed around him" (9:3). The description makes it appear that the light was something like a lightning bolt. The text does not say that the light continued to shine, nor does the text say that those who were with him did not see it. We are told that no one else except Saul heard a voice. The effect of the sudden explosion of light from the skies was to knock Saul and his companions to the

> *Read Acts 9:1-9. What especially intrigues you about this Scripture? What questions does it raise for you? What would be the response to such an experience in the contemporary world?*

road (26:13). While lying in the road, Saul had a conversation with Jesus. Jesus initiated the dialogue by asking, "Saul, Saul, why do you persecute me?" (9:4).

Saul responded, "Who are you, Lord?" (verse 5)—answering his own question. Jesus said, "I am Jesus, whom you are persecuting. But get up and enter the city, and you will be told what you are to do" (verses 5-6).

Saul would later recount to Herod that Jesus told him that his mission would now be to evangelize rather than to terrorize: "I have appeared to you for this purpose, to appoint you to serve and testify to the things in which you have seen me and to those in which I will appear to you. I will rescue you from your people and from the Gentiles—to whom I am sending you to open their eyes so that they may turn from darkness to light and from the power of Satan to God, so that they may receive forgiveness of sins and a place among those who are sanctified by faith in me" (26:16-18).

Saul was transformed. He did not know what was ahead for him, but he was a different man. He had a chat with Jesus, whom he had believed to be dead; and he called that same Jesus "Lord." As he rose from the ground, he could see nothing, although his eyes were open.

In this condition, then, Saul was led by the hand into the city where he was taken to the house of Judas on Straight Street. At this point, we observe a transformation in another character in the story: Ananias. God spoke to Ananias and told him of Saul's whereabouts and directed him to go to the house of Judas to pray for him (9:11-12). Ananias, identified as a disciple (verse 10) and as a "devout man according to the law and well spoken of by all the Jews living there (22:12), was understandably wary. "Lord, I have heard from many about this man, how much evil he has done to your saints in Jerusalem; and here he has authority from the chief priests to bind all who invoke your name" (9:13-14). The Lord reassured him, saying that Saul "is an instrument whom I have chosen to bring my name before Gentiles" (verse 15).

So Ananias moved out of his comfort zone and went to the house of Judas, where he was led to Saul. Ananias prayed for him, incredibly calling him "brother." Immediately, Saul was able to see. He got up and was baptized, and he began to eat again. After three days of no food or water (verse 9), he must have been weak.

Paul Entered the Witness Protection Program

Well, not really. However, he did receive a new name and a new job. For a while, no one seemed to know where he was, and the bad guys could not get to him. His Hebrew name was *Saul*; but Luke, the author of Acts, begins to refer to him by his Roman name, *Paul*, beginning in Acts 13:9. Thereafter, Luke identifies Saul as Paul, as indeed Paul does in his letter to various churches later in life.

Read Acts 9:19-31. Create a before and after list of Paul. If like to draw, create a before and after portrait of Paul. What, if anything, about Paul remained the same? What personality traits do you think served him well after the experience on the road to Damascus? How do you see the role of the early Christian community in the conversion experience?

The immediate task for Paul was to get out of Damascus without being killed by his former friends, who now considered him a turncoat. They had undercovered people watching all the gates of the city, ready to catch him if he attempted to flee. His new friends, however, found an "opening in the wall" and lowered him in a basket so that he was able to escape to freedom (9:23-25). Paul later showed up in Jerusalem—how much later, we are not sure. The disciples were still uncertain about Paul; but he was befriended by Barnabas, who would appear later in our story and become Paul's traveling friend.

Are You Ready For an Ambush Makeover?

Perhaps one lesson to draw from this is that transformation can take different forms. There is no one-size-fits-all approach to how change takes place in our lives on our spiritual journey. Clearly, there were immediate differences in Paul's life. He stopped killing people. That is huge.

Immediately after his transformation, Paul's skills were put to use for different purposes. "For several days he was with the disciples in Damascus, and immediately he began to proclaim Jesus in the synagogues, saying, 'He is the Son of God.' All who heard him were amazed and said, 'Is not this the man who made havoc in Jerusalem among those who invoked this name? And has he not come here for the purpose of bringing them bound before the chief priests?' Saul became increasingly more powerful and confounded the Jews who lived in Damascus by proving that Jesus was the Messiah" (9:20-22).

Such radical and immediate transformation is not unusual. We reach critical mass and suddenly have the power to initiate the change we have always wanted to make.

> *Who in your life has had a radical transformation?*

The doctor says you experienced an atrial fibrillation, and suddenly your lifestyle and eating habits change.

Chuck Colson was part of the Watergate scandal in the 1970s and living a life without God. He went to prison, experienced a conversion, and has been an active voice in the Christian community and a strong advocate for prison reform for the past 25 years.

Jeb Macgruder was also part of the Nixon inner circle that was exposed during the scandal. He did prison time and then did seminary time and became a Presbyterian minister.

John DeLorean, erstwhile car designer and millionaire cocaine dealer, was born again.

Bob Dylan has had a number of "conversions" going through a "born again" phase.

Martin Luther had his own "Damascus road" experience on a road during a frightening storm, went to the monastery, and found Romans

1:17: "The one who is righteous will live by faith." And the Reformation began.

Augustine was running from God until he heard a voice while meditating in a garden in Milan: *"Tolle, lege."* Take it and read. He picked up Romans 13, and the light dawned. He became one of the greatest apologists of the faith the church has known.

These accounts all describe a radical transformation. Yet, not all transformations are experienced in crisis. Some are more of a gradual metamorphosis than an instant makeover.

The purpose of Paul's transformation was to make him a transformer of others. Wherever he went, he changed things, upset the status quo. He had become a true believer and was not afraid to share his faith. Paul was ambushed on the road to Damascus, and the makeover began. We do not need to be ambushed; we simply need the will to change and the perseverance to see it through. That is something God and this community of faith we call the church is all about.

CLOSING WORSHIP

Turn off the lights in the room. If possible, turn on a lamp or a flashlight and train it on the center of the group. Let this represent the light from heaven on the road to Damascus. Let it also represent the light that God wants us to see so that we, in partnership with God, can make the changes we need to make. Reflect on this concept silently for a few minutes. Then close with the prayer of Saint Francis:

Lord, make me an instrument of Your peace.
Where there is hatred, let me sow love;
where there is injury, pardon;
where there is doubt, faith;
where there is despair, hope;
where there is darkness, light;
and where there is sadness, joy.
O, Divine Master,
grant that I may not so much seek
to be consoled as to console;
to be understood as to understand;
to be loved as to love
for it is in giving that we receive;
it is in pardoning that we are pardoned;
and it is in dying that we are born to eternal life.
Amen.

[1]From "Get Rid of Your Scary Clothes!" by Linda Stasi in *The New York Post,* August 27, 2003 (*nypost.com*) and *What Not to Wear* at *bbcamerica.com*.

Session 6

WORKING TOGETHER IN MINISTRY

Acts 16:18–19:10

This session explores the ministries of Lydia and of Priscilla and Aquila in order to identify ways to work together for Christ. It will provide opportunities to develop ministries that offer hospitality and service in our contemporary world.

GATHERING

Light a candle. Consider ways we welcome one another. What do you do to make people feel welcome in your home, church, school, or business? Pray together a prayer that invites and welcomes the presence of God during your study.

Built for Hospitality

If you own a home built in the early 1900s, a Victorian house, for example, you have a house that was built for social occasions. The parlor, often with an upright piano in it, was designed to receive visitors that—in pre-telephone America—you most surely

68

would have had. Stopping by, or dropping in, was a part of the social landscape. Formal visitors, of course, were not expected to stay more than 30 minutes; and they never removed their coats. However, dropping in was something people did all the time and, in fact, was something people were expected to do. Absent the technological devices of today (such as e-mail, cell phones, IMing, and Web cams), visiting was the social glue that held a community together. The parlor, from the Old French *parler*, meaning "to speak," was a place for communication, chit-chat, appointments, and courtship.

> *Test the hypothesis advanced in the last paragraph. Do we drop by these days? If so, when was the last time and what was the purpose of the visit? Can you recall the last time someone dropped by to visit you? Do your relatives do this? neighbors?*

Hospitality has not entirely disappeared, especially in rural America. Peter Panagore, a pastor who lives near Deer Isle, off the rural coast in Downeast, Maine, says that a neighbor in his community is still expected to take the time to chat when an unexpected visitor drops by the house or stops in at the post office or taps you on your shoulder in the canned goods aisle of The Galley grocer.

"It is part of the island charm," Panagore says, "but it is also necessary for survival." Visiting is how news of island happenings travels. It is how you find out whose boat sunk in the last blow or whose house burned down; and once that has been established, the islanders can figure out how to help.

Such help is not limited to churchgoers. Even the non-churched believe it is their "Christian" duty to render assistance. It does not matter whether you have been on the island 20 years or two years; everyone pitches in to help, because, as the expression goes, a good tide raises everybody's boats together.

Today, we not only do not expect people to drop by, we do not want them to! Dropping by is not something we are likely to do ourselves. No way are we just going to show up at someone's door for a chat.

Biblical Hospitality

The idea of hospitality is deeply ingrained in Scripture as it was in the ancient world. God is pictured in the Old Testament as host and God's people as guests. "For I am your passing guest, / an alien, like all my forebears" (Psalm 39:12). Israel was an alien nation for much of its history. It was dependent on God for protection and help. This is most clearly seen when Israel, after its Exodus, is dependent on the daily mercies of God for its very survival. Such literal dependence was to signal their spiritual dependence and need of God as well.

Abraham's generosity in entertaining strangers is noted in Genesis 18:2-8. This theme of offering lodging, protection, food, and clothing to the alien or stranger is an important one in Scripture. As aliens in a strange culture, such travelers often needed immediate assistance. Moreover, widows, orphans, and the poor were often without a means of making a living since they lacked community and family standing that might provide a home, land, or an inheritance. These people's survival depended on the hospitality of neighbors and strangers.

Perhaps the centerpiece of ancient hospitality was the common meal. To share a meal was to share a life; and this, therefore, was how friendships were born and nurtured and how the bonds of friendship were forged.

You can imagine then the shock to the community when Jesus ate his meals with tax collectors, "publicans and sinners." The culture was inclined to extend hospitality, but there were limits. That Jesus would signal his friendship and solidarity with these, the least among them, was scandalous then as it would be today.

There are other meals mentioned in the New Testament. Jesus' feeding of the 5,000 places him in the position of host. The last supper meal Jesus had with his disciples, Jesus' post-resurrection meals, Peter's meal with the Gentiles (Acts 10:48–11:3), and the meals of the early church (Acts 2:42-47) all point to the importance of hospitality in the culture of Jesus' day. Holy Communion is a "meal" in which the

> *Form three teams. Each team choose one of the following Scriptures: Genesis 18:2-8; John 13:1-13; and Acts 2:42-47. Read the Scripture together. What does it say to you about hospitality?*

faith community is gathered about a table, often called "the Lord's Table." In gathering about this table, we signal our connection and oneness with each other.

Lydia's Witness of Hospitality

In Acts 16, the first thing Lydia does when she responds to Paul's message is to invite people over. The ancient world lived with a culture of hospitality firmly in place, yet Paul was often reluctant to receive hospitality. Stung by accusations that he might have abused the hospitality of others, Paul usually insisted on paying his own way and providing for his own needs (1 Corinthians 4:11-12; 2 Corinthians 11:9; 1 Thessalonians 2:9). However, when Lydia, a "worshiper of God" (Acts 16:14) received Paul's message and was baptized, it was hard for him to refuse her suggestion. A refusal was made especially difficult since Lydia prefaced her invitation by saying, "If you have judged me to be faithful to the Lord . . ." (verse 15). No wonder the Scripture notes, "And she prevailed upon us" (verse 15).

Lydia was from the city of Thyatira (verse 14) in the province of Lydia (from whence she may have gotten her name) in what is today western Turkey. Today, the location is occupied by the city of Akhisar. Only 42 miles inland from the Aegean Sea, it was a city known for its craft and trade guilds, such as bakers, bronze smiths, wool workers, potters, linen weavers, and tanners, and was therefore a city in which, as a seller of purple, Lydia might have been active. The cloth she sold was of the most expensive type available, and it was dyed with the dye from the so-called purple "madder" plant that grew profusely around Thyatira. As head of the household and a woman of means, Lydia was particularly able to support the early church with her hospitality. Her hospitality was and continues to be a strong witness for the value of Christian community.

> Read Acts 16. Note especially verse 40. How do you think Lydia's witness of hospitality was important to Paul's ministry?

What Happened to the Guest Room?

The church has always understood the need to extend hospitality to the stranger. During the 19th century, there was a growing awareness that if the kingdom of God was to be ushered into the world, Christians needed to get their act together and start to bring it about.

One of the most influential books of the era was not a scholarly tome but a pulp fiction novel written by a pastor named Charles Sheldon. *In His Steps* recounted the reaction of a congregation when an indigent beggar walked into their morning service one Sunday morning. The WWJD bracelets kids wear these days is the grandchild of the central question posed by Sheldon's book: What would we do if we walked in his steps? During the time of the itinerant—often Methodist—preachers who traveled by horseback, a network of homes developed along the way known as Shunammite homes. In these homes, the weary and saddle-sore preacher received a welcome and a place to lay his head for the night. (For the story of the Shunammite woman, see 2 Kings 4:8-17.) The preacher's room for the night was often referred to as a "prophet's chamber," and it was a place to rest and be renewed.[1]

The spirit of hospitality extended far beyond the religious world, however. Most homes built then and through much of the 20th century included a guest room. Visiting relatives or friends who were traveling on a network of federal two-lane highways prior to the development of the interstate system, often planned their trip in terms of the stops they could make with friends who had "room at the inn" for a night or two. Today, the guest room has fallen out of favor.

How do you accommodate houseguests? Do you have a guest room? a formal dining room? a living room? How does your house or apartment provide areas for hospitality?

Homeowners would rather have a media room than a guest room. The dining room where communal meals were served is also disappearing, as is a living room, now replaced by the family room. We have neither the time nor the energy to prepare a meal for ourselves, let alone others; and it is easier to order pizza and eat it in the kitchen or on the run. As for anyone staying the night—who would want to do that? We value privacy today, and so we do not want to stay in someone else's home; and we are not eager to entertain anyone else in our own home either.

> *How do you think Christians can extend hospitality today?*

There are sociological reasons for all of this, of course. Family and friends may be houseguests, but we are reluctant to invite a total stranger into the house in this day of registered sex offenders and a high crime rate. This is only prudent. So how does a Christian extend hospitality today? How can we be obedient to the biblical command to befriend and take in the "alien and stranger"? Is it critical that hospitality be understood as entertaining the stranger, the marginalized, the oppressed, within our habitats?

Hospitality: Inside Out

The biblical hospitality requirement is equally met when the arrow is from in to out. While hospitality certainly can be practiced from outside to inside our homes, another option is for us to move inside out and meet people where they are. Christians have found many ways to practice such hospitality. Christian groups are helping illegal aliens who are in danger of perishing in the desert in their attempt to get into this country. Whatever your position on immigration, you take a Samaritan approach and help the man left for dead. Many churches have their own food banks or help in the serving and distribution of food at a local agency. Others have found ways to clothe people, provide job skills, and support battered women. Some churches have taken sandwiches down to the inner city and distributed them on certain noon hours of the month.

> *Discuss the concept of taking "home" to the stranger. How might we do this? Make a list of specific actions that individuals or churches could do to offer hospitality to the stranger.*

If we are to be judged as true believers—to use Lydia's language—then we must find ways to open our homes and our hearts. While in many cases we

73

cannot open our homes today, we can take "home" to those who are homeless and hungry.

The Swimmy principle

Leo Lionni tells the story of a little fish named Swimmy in an illustrated children's book named after the central character.[2] Swimmy is just one of many other minnows in a school of minnows swimming about, except for one thing: While the other minnows are all reddish-gold, Swimmy is pure black.

Usually the school of fish swims along peacefully enough, but sometimes a larger predator fish comes along. Then, in a flash, all the fish, including Swimmy, scatter. Swimmy begins to think about this and does not believe it is fair that the big fish should intimidate, bully—and eat—the little fish. Yet, what could one tiny misfit fish do about that?

Suddenly Swimmy has a brilliant idea. It is a plan that celebrates his own unique style—his solid black coloring—and depends on the cooperative teamwork of all his minnow schoolmates. Swimmy organizes the school of all his friends so that they are swimming in the shape of a large fish. Swimmy himself, his dark body flashing, creates the "eye" of this illusionary giant fish.

In the last scene of the book, we see a huge would-be predator take one look at this intimidating mammoth and then turn tail and run!

The apostle Paul must have felt like Swimmy on a number of occasions. He was always running into predators, as it were. After his conversion, his former friends tried to kill him. On his first trip into what is now central Turkey, he and his fellow minnow missionary, Barnabas, were stoned and left for dead. In Philippi, he and Silas were beaten and thrown into prison. He led a harrowing life and details it more fully in 1 Corinthians 4:9-13 and 2 Corinthians 11:23-33. At times he felt like "the scum of the earth" (1 Corinthians 4:13, NIV); and he

> *Think of people who use their secular work to support their real interest in ministry. What are the pros and cons of having a bivocational pastor (one who earns a living with a secular job Monday-Friday and serves a church on Sunday)?*

asserts that he had "worked much harder, been in prison more frequently, been flogged more severely, and been exposed to death again and again" more than any of his colleagues (2 Corinthians 11:23, NIV).

How does work get done at home? at the office? at church? Describe your attitude toward the person who tries to do it all himself or herself? Does your church have boards, committees, or teams? What is the difference? Do you prefer to work alone or work in a team? Make a list of some of the problems that can keep Christians from working together harmoniously.

However, Paul, like Jesus, who sent out the disciples two by two, believed in the power of teamwork. He usually traveled and ministered with someone else. In Corinth, the team expanded. Aquila and Priscilla arrived in Corinth fresh from Rome, leaving the Eternal City because the emperor had ordered them and the entire Jewish community to do so. Paul welcomed the help and the friendship. Since Priscilla and Aquila were tentmakers like him, Paul plied his trade with them as a means of earning a living in order to pursue his real ministry, telling others the good news.

The three of them, joined later by an Alexandrian Jew named Apollos, form a strong team to advance the gospel and provide some measure of protection in this hostile, cosmopolitan city from those who objected to his work.

It is not always easy to work in teams and to share leadership. However, Paul was a strong advocate of shared responsibilities and urged his co-workers to minister in the particular area in which God had given them a passion, a gift, a charisma. He often used the metaphor of the body, which can only be considered healthy if every part, however important or slight, is functioning harmoniously for the benefit of the whole.

Paul knew that for the gospel to go forward effectively in a hostile culture, he needed to get the right people on the bus; and Aquila and Priscilla and Apollos fit the bill. Actually, the bus metaphor refers to a device used by Jim Collins in *From Good to Great*. In one chapter, he reveals that Level 5 leaders, the great ones, do not know at first where the bus is headed but work hard on getting the right people on the bus.

Not only that, they get the right people in the right seats on the bus. Then, and only then, the team can decide where the bus is going.[3] Paul seemed to know where the bus was headed, but he needed the right people in the right seats to get the bus going.

This is in contrast to the way it often works in the local church. We are often less concerned about getting the right people on the bus as we are with just getting anyone on the bus. "You want to teach Sunday school? Great!"

Back to School

As much as we may value teamwork, we are often suspicious of it. That may be because when we worked on teams in the past, we ended up doing most of the work. Teams suffer when some team members do not carry their weight. So we fall back on the old notion that if something is going to be done right, we had better do it ourselves.

Perhaps it is time to go back to Swimmy's school. It is time to rejoin our fishmates and come together to create a larger, sleeker, and more powerful swimming machine. To do this, we might keep some things in mind.

First, if we are not passionate about our role, we might as well forget it. God's work suffers and we do, too, if we are square pegs smashed into round holes. Marcus Buckingham and Donald Clifton, in *Now, Discover Your Strengths*, argue that any type of cooperative effort, whether it is a church or a corporation, must be built on a strength-based approach or it is doomed to failure. The task is to determine what our passions are and build ministry around those passions.[4]

Second, we must be willing to move from "tour guide to traveler," according to Spencer Burke in *Making Sense of the Church*. The "tour guide" style of leadership is characterized by a "bang-the-drum" kind of leader who gathers everyone around and then sallies forth into the world. The tour guide approach is hierarchical: senior pastors, associate pastors, and on down to the minnows. A better approach is the "traveler" motif in which our leaders travel with us in our faith and mission journey. This approach puts us "on the way" with everyone else in one big school. We learn, pray, struggle, and succeed together.[5]

Finally, the team must decide what it is all about. For Swimmy, it was about survival—trying to avoid getting eaten by the big fish. What is it about for us?

CLOSING WORSHIP

Cut sheets of construction paper into the shape of small fish. Write on each fish a word that describes your strongest attribute. Do this in silence. Place your fish on the worship center. Thank God for the gifts God has given the church. Close by praying together the Lord's Prayer.

[1]From "Help Wanted: Only Shunammites Need Apply," by Len Sweet in *Homiletics,* July 19, 1992.

[2]From *Swimmy,* by Leo Lionni (Dragofly Books, 1973).

[3]From *From Good to Great;* page 47.

[4]From *Now, Discover Your Strengths,* by Marcus Buckingham and Donald O. Clifton (The Free Press, 2001).

[5]From *Making Sense of the Church: Eavesdropping on Emerging Conversations About God, Community, and Culture,* by Spencer Burke (Zondervan, 2003); page 35.

Session

7

PAUL'S FAREWELL

Acts 20:17-38

This session explores the strong sense of community and bonding that is expressed in Paul's farewell to the elders at Ephesus. It will help us identify and celebrate sources of support in our own communities of faith and how we help one another through difficult times.

GATHERING

Light a candle. Read the purpose statement above. Share briefly the last "goodbye" experience you had. What emotions did you experience then, and how have those emotions changed since? In the prayer, ask God to show you how we can support each other through our goodbye moments.

cya!

You could argue that the so-called "death of distance" has resulted in a dearth, if not death, of goodbyes. Who really says goodbye anymore? We are more likely to say "cya" ("see ya") at the end of an IM conversation with friends in New Dehli, in Singapore, or down the street. We set up our Web cams and voice conversations and can talk pixel to pixel with grandchildren or professional colleagues. We do not say goodbye anymore.

> *What other goodbye moments would you add to the list?*

Or so it seems. The truth is that we experience many goodbye moments in our lives. We say goodbye to our child when he or she goes on a military mission. We say goodbye when our pastor leaves for another city. We say goodbye when our mother or father is in the last stages of cancer. We say goodbye when our marriage has been shattered on the rocks of indifference, animosity, infidelity, or thoughtlessness. We say goodbye when a child zooms off to college five states away.

Paul's Goodbye

The apostle Paul had a major goodbye moment in Acts 20:17-38. He had been with this congregation at Ephesus for at least two years (19:10); and after a brief journey of a few months in Macedonia and Greece, he was heading for Jerusalem where his arrest was certain, as was his transfer to Rome and probable execution (21:10-14).

So eager was Paul to get to Jerusalem, that he felt he could not spare the time to visit Ephesus. Instead, he sent word to have the elders of the church meet him at Miletus, the harbor serving Ephesus and the southwestern area of Asia Minor, where he was about to board the boat for the next leg of the journey.

In the ancient world, there were, of course, no cell phones allowing anyone to chat conveniently, no telephones of any kind. There was no form of communication except letters, and those often took months to arrive at their destination. A farewell in the ancient world was of much greater cultural significance than it is today. The farewell address had become an embedded and familiar cultural ritual, and it is seen frequently in Scripture. The farewell of Moses is recorded beginning in Deuteronomy 29. The high point is his declaration: "See, I have set before you today life and prosperity, death and adversity" (30:15). Joshua, Moses' successor, likewise, said goodbye; and his farewell advice was the well-known charge to "choose this day whom you will serve. . . . but as for me and my household, we will serve the LORD"

> *Read the goodbye moments in the following Scriptures: Deuteronomy 30:15; Joshua 24:15, 1 Samuel 12:24; and 2 Timothy 4:7. What seems most significant to you in these Scriptures?*

(Joshua 24:15). Samuel's last word of advice to the new nation of Israel and Saul its king is to "fear the LORD, and serve him faithfully with all your heart; for consider what great things he has done for you" (1 Samuel 12:24). Second Peter could also be considered a farewell address. Then there is the poignant text of Paul's second letter to Timothy, shortly before his execution, in which he tells Timothy that "I have fought the good fight, I have finished the race, I have kept the faith" (2 Timothy 4:7).

For Paul, the elders at Ephesus, and the people of the day, saying goodbye meant not seeing one's face again: "Now I know that none of you, among whom I have gone about proclaiming the kingdom, will ever see my face again" (Acts 20:25). When there is a chance or certainty that we will not see someone again, we do not say, "cya." We say, "Goodbye"; and it may be the hardest thing we ever do.

Paul Turns to His Colleagues for Support

How do we do this? What resources are available to us during sad transitions in our lives? To answer these questions, let us first look at Paul's experience with the elders of Ephesus and how his experience can help us today.

It is helpful to note that Paul's relationship to his co-workers and those he had nurtured in the faith were important to him. He did not just go sailing by Ephesus. He stopped and specifically requested a meeting. This was no doubt as much for his benefit as it was for theirs. Paul needed their support, love, and understanding. How hard is it today to request a meeting for the purpose of seeking support, love, and prayers? I suspect that it is difficult for people to be that open and

> *Read Acts 20:19-38. What do you see as the most significant content of Paul's farewell?*

vulnerable today, to say to their co-workers, friends, and spiritual companions: "Hey, let's have a meeting. I need you right now in my life. Let's pray." Yet Paul, whose spiritual strength and wisdom is a model for us all, who towers as

80

a giant in the hall of fame of saints, requested such a meeting. He sent out a call for help. Paul needed to see these people one more time.

Paul was strong on the body as a metaphor for how the church functions. When one part of the body suffers, the rest of the body suffers as well. We laugh together, and we cry together. That is how it should be. Paul needed time with his friends and colleagues before leaving. When they arrived, he spoke to them in an address that contains three components: a summary of his past, suggestions for the future, and a prayer. These actions could help us in our goodbye moments.

Paul's Life Summary (Acts 20:18-24, 33-35)

Paul outlined what he believed were the important features of his work with the Ephesian community. He served the Lord with humility (Acts 20:19). Paul could have boasted of his accomplishments; he could have adopted a superior attitude toward those with whom he ministered, but he did not do so. How important is humility as a trait in leaders? Most great leaders are people marked by extraordinary humility. According to Jim Collins, Level 5 leaders have no shortage of ambition; but it is ambition for the company, or the mission; and they have little interest in promoting themselves.[1] Paul was like this.

Paul served with tears (verse 19). He was human, not a machine. He was a person who could feel the pain of others. He served the Lord with passion and energy. It was a key to his effectiveness as a leader. He experienced the fullness of the human condition right along with everyone else, and he was not embarrassed to admit it.

Paul preached publicly and privately (verse 20). His public preaching took place outdoors, in the synagogues, and in the marketplace. Paul's private preaching took place, no doubt, in the homes of people in the community. His ministry was focused on preaching the good news. He preached to everyone, Jews and Gentiles alike, even though both groups often gave him a hard time. Paul did not mince words. He said that they must have "repentance toward God" (verse 21).

Paul did not consider his life "of any value" (verse 24). He said this in light of the suffering and hardships that had been forecast for him. Paul knew he would surely be arrested in Jerusalem. He was facing a difficult time, but what he really wanted to do was to "finish [his] course and the ministry that [he] received from the Lord Jesus" (verse 24). Seen in this light, Paul's mere physical life had no value in and of itself. In an age where we are attempting to lengthen life, clone life, party hard, and live long, to hear someone say, "I do not count my life of any value to myself" sounds unrealistic.

Paul did not covet silver or gold (verse 33); he paid his own way (verse 34). This was not about the money. Imagine the commentary Paul might have for some so-called evangelists today, the "name-it-and-claim-it" charlatans of television. The apostle was sensitive to charges that he took advantage of the generosity of others. When Priscilla and Aquila came to Corinth, Paul worked with them, plying his trade as a tentmaker.

In his final words to his friends, Paul reminded them that his interest in them was completely sincere. He held up his hands to them and said, "You know for yourselves that I worked with my own hands to support myself and my companions" (verse 34). This policy, he said, was designed to encourage them to see that "by such work we must support the weak, remembering the words of the Lord Jesus, for he himself said, 'It is more blessed to give than to receive'" (verse 35).

His comments here reflect a life that was directed outward to others and upward to God. He served God with humility, and he was tireless in his efforts to minister in the community.

Paul's Suggestions for the Future

> *Pretend that you are about to leave on a long trip, perhaps a dangerous trip; or imagine that you are near the end of your life. Summarize who you are and what you are all about. Write what you imagine in a letter to your friends and family. What gives you a sense of value? joy? What, if anything, would you do differently?*

After Paul summarizes his life, he moves into a short rehearsal of how the elders at Ephesus should behave after his departure, which meant that he was not only taking leave of Ephesus, but of life. His advice? "Keep watch over yourselves and over all the flock, of which the Holy Spirit has made you overseers" (verse 28).

People who say goodbye often have last words before they leave. In Shakespeare's play *Hamlet*, Polonius shares the parting words of Polonius with his son, Laertes, before Laertes leaves for the continent. His speech includes the well-known phrases "neither a borrower nor a lender be" and "to thine own self be true, / and it must follow, as the night the day, / thou canst not then be false to any man."

> *What words of care, advice, or watchfulness are you most likely to offer to colleagues at work, to friends, or to family?*

At our house, it is not quite so prosaic when our grown children leave to return to their own homes. When they pull out of the driveway, we usually shout: "Drive safe!" When we say goodbye, our last words may be "I love you"; but more often than not, our last words at departure are suggestive, protective, and instructive: "Drive safe!"

Paul's last words to his friends in Ephesus were of the "drive safe" variety. They were to keep watch over themselves first and then over others—sort of like the flight attendant's instruction to put the oxygen mask on yourself first before trying to put one on the baby. Paul described this "watching" by using the Greek word *episkopos*, from which we get our word *bishop*. It is a compound word: *skopos* from *skopio*, meaning "to look," and *epi*, meaning "over." So a bishop is one who "looks over" or "keeps watch over." Good leaders are good bishops. They are people who watch over themselves diligently before assuming that they are fit to watch over others, especially the flock of God.

Paul's Prayer

When I was growing up and Dad had to leave on a trip or we had a missionary visiting with us, we always stopped to pray just before departure. The prayer always included a request for God to give us "journeying mercies." We are not sure what Paul said in his prayer. No doubt he reviewed much of what he had already told them. They might have prayed for "journeying mercies" for Paul. We know there was not a dry eye in the place. It was a weepy affair: "There was much weeping among them all; they embraced Paul and kissed him, grieving especially because of what he had said, that they would not see him again" (verses 37-38). In any case, there is nothing like praying together when we have to part with each other, regardless of the cause of the parting.

Bonhoeffer Sails Home

> Write a one-sentence goodbye prayer for a goodbye moment you or someone you know has experienced. Save the sentence prayer for use in the closing prayer activity.

A little more than 60 years ago, the Nazis executed German theologian Dietrich Bonheoffer in a prison camp at Flossenberg for his role in an assassination plot against Hitler. Bonhoeffer died in April of 1945, only days before the war's end. He was 39.

A brilliant theologian, Bonhoeffer had visited Union Theological Seminary in New York City in the 1930s. Back in Germany, the situation was getting desperate. Hitler was systematically cleansing the country of Jews, homosexuals, gypsies, and the disabled. The church was not wringing its hands; it was sitting on its hands. Bonhoeffer became restless in New York. Finally, he decided he needed to return to Germany and be part of the struggle of the Confessing Church, a small alliance of churches determined to resist the regime.

Bonhoeffer's friends in New York, like Paul's in Ephesus, urged him not to go. They told him it was too dangerous, but Bonhoeffer was determined to say goodbye. He thought that he needed to stand with his country during its present suffering if he was to participate in its future rebuilding. He left New York and sailed to his "Jerusalem" and ultimately his "Rome" but not before leaving behind, like Paul, a brilliant example of how—even in the pathos of separation—to keep his heart, soul, and mind clear.[2] Bonhoeffer knew the importance of understanding his life work, of working on a vision for the future, and of praying his way through a problem. He also knew that the effectiveness of these three components was multiplied exponentially when the community of faith was factored in.

The Bislett Effect

People who run world-class races know about Bislett Stadium in Oslo, Norway. This is a stadium where 62 track and field records have been broken over the past 50 years or so. No other track can boast of such a record for record-breaking achievements. Why? The crowd. The track is narrow, with only six lanes; and the grandstand is so steep that the fans are practically on top of the runners. When you have 21,000 maniacs screaming at you, their energy practically pushes you across the finish line. Call it the home field advantage or the Bislett effect. It is real, and it is crucial in our life journey.

When we come to transitions in our lives—though perhaps not as dramatic as Paul's experiences or Dietrich Bonhoeffer's trials—community support can make all the difference. It is good to have an arena of cheering, praying, laughing, weeping, or hugging people who are traveling on this journey with us and part of this community. Together we will help one another to get across the finish line, wherever that line is and through whatever struggle it may take to get there.

CLOSING WORSHIP

Write a group prayer using the sentence prayers created earlier. The prayer could take the form of a litany with a recurring response. With the entire group, go through the three steps the apostle Paul followed in his farewell in terms of the group experience. Summarize what has been accomplished in this study. Then discuss how the study might have changed your attitudes and behaviors for the future. Close the session with the group prayer that you have written.

[1]From *Performing the Faith: Bonhoeffer and the Practice of Nonviolence*, by Stanley Hauerwas (Brazos Press, 2004); pages 33-72.

[2]From *Performing the Faith;* pages 33-72.

Appendix

Background Scriptures for "Community: You Will Be My Witnesses"

Acts 2:1-42, 47
Acts 4:32-35
Acts 3:1–4:1-31
Acts 6:8–7:60
Acts 8:4-40

Acts 1:1-48
Acts 12:1-17
Acts 9:1-31
Acts 16:18–19:10
Acts 20:17-38

The Committee on the Uniform Series

The Committee on the Uniform Series (CUS) is made up of persons appointed by their respective denominations, which, although differing in certain elements of faith and polity, hold a common faith in Jesus Christ, the Son of God, as Lord and Savior, whose saving gospel is to be taught to all humankind. CUS has about 70 members who represent 19 Protestant denominations in the US and Canada, who work together to develop the International Bible Lessons for Christian Teaching. A team from this committee develops the cycles of Scriptures and themes that form the backbone of the Bible lesson development guides. The cycles present a balance between Old and New Testaments, although the weight is on the latter. Cycles through 2016 are organized around the following themes: creation, call, covenant, Christ, community, commitment, God, hope, worship, tradition, faith, and justice.

—MARVIN CROPSEY,
Chair, Committee on the Uniform Series

Other Bible Study Resources

If your group would like to explore a long-term Bible study, we recommend:

The Jesus Collection. A series of books about the life, teachings, and ministry of Jesus Christ, each of which invites the reader into renewal and commitment.

The Life and Letters of Paul Series. Historical, archaeological, and geographic data interwoven into a fascinating study of Paul's epistles. Each book takes an in-depth look at particular aspects of Paul's ministry as illuminated in his letters.

The FaithQuestions Series. Offers studies of issues in theology, ethics, missions, biblical interpretation, and church history. Designed for adults who seek a deeper engagement with the Christian faith and with Scripture.

If your group would like to study other short-term small-group resources, we suggest the following:

Adult Bible Study. Published quarterly. Thirteen lessons per quarter. Bible study resources based on the International Lesson Series. Also known as the Uniform Series.

Genesis to Revelation. A comprehensive study based on the New International Version of the Bible. Twenty-four volumes. Thirteen sessions per volume.

Journey Through the Bible. A comprehensive study based on the New Revised Standard Version of the Bible. Sixteen volumes. Thirteen sessions per volume.

DISCIPLE Bible Study. A 34-week foundation study of the Bible in which participants learn how to become more effective disciples through Bible study.